A Student's Vocabulary for

BIBLICAL HEBREW AND ARAMAIC

Larry A. Mitchel

D0224044

A Student's Vocabulary for

BIBLICAL HEBREW AND ARAMAIC

Larry A. Mitchel

Academie
Books Grand Rapids,
Michigan
Zondervan Publishing House

A STUDENT'S VOCABULARY FOR BIBLICAL HEBREW AND ARAMAIC
Copyright © 1984 by The Zondervan Corporation
Grand Rapids, Michigan

ACADEMIE BOOKS is an imprint of Zondervan Publishing House,
1415 Lake Drive, S.E., Grand Rapids, Michigan 49506

Library of Congress Cataloging in Publication Data

Mitchel, Larry A.
    A student's vocabulary for biblical Hebrew and Aramaic.

    Bibliography: p.
    Includes index.
    1. Hebrew language—Word frequency.   2. Hebrew language—
Glossaries, vocabularies, etc.   3. Aramaic language—
Glossaries, vocabularies, etc.   4. Bible.   O.T.—
Language, style.   I. Title.
PJ4845.M5   1984   221.4'4   84-5219
ISBN 0-310-45461-1

All rights reserved. No part of this publication may be reproduced, stored in a retrieval system, or transmitted in any form or by any means— electronic, mechanical, photocopy, recording, or any other—except for brief quotations in printed reviews, without the prior permission of the publisher.

Printed in the United States of America

88 89 90 91 — 10 9 8 7 6 5

To Leona Glidden Running for whom

Semitic languages are a consuming and

contagious interest.

CONTENTS

PREFACE

Purpose of this *Student's Vocabulary*

In light of the availability of a number of Hebrew vocabulary lists, it is proper to ask why another such list should be put in print. The volumes that first come to mind each make a real contribution. George M. Landes's *A Student's Vocabulary of Biblical Hebrew* has an obvious advantage in its grouping of Hebrew words by root, a helpful aid in learning vocabulary. The *Hebrew Vocabularies* of J. Barton Payne present the Hebrew particles in a particularly helpful way. And the small volume by John D. W. Watts (*Lists of Words Occurring Frequently in the Hebrew Bible.*), which like Payne's is based on William Rainey Harper's *Hebrew Vocabularies* (published in 1890), presents Hebrew vocabulary down to 25 occurrences in a very compact form.

However, in my experience in teaching biblical Hebrew on the undergraduate level, I have felt that each of the above excellent works have presented two fundamental problems for entry-level Hebrew students: (1) each volume incorporates a number of separate lists, requiring reference to various parts of the book in order to find all Hebrew words of a given frequency; and (2) the lists themselves are apparently set by somewhat arbitrary word-frequency limits, resulting in lists of greatly variable length. The present work seeks to remedy both of those basic problems.

The lexicon of Old Testament Hebrew contains some 10,000 words in all. Of these, approximately 740 occur fifty times or more. A full 490 occur as *hapax legomena* by Harold R. Cohen's definition (see volume in Bibliography; pages xv and 6-7). Many more words in the MT occur only once, though other occurrences of that same Hebrew root may also appear.

The Aramaic lexicon consists of approximately 650 words. Since the amount of Aramaic text in the OT is so much less than that of Hebrew text, the number of occurrences of Aramaic words is lower.

For the Hebrew vocabulary sections (Sections 1-5) an attempt has been made to include every word that occurs ten times or more. The one exception to this inclusive statement has to do with proper nouns: only those personal and place names that are used fifty times or more are included. The primary reason for including proper nouns at all is that while some Hebrew place names and personal names are reasonably "transparent" to students familiar with the OT in English translation, many are rather "opaque." This is the case because the English transliteration that the student knows often reflects Greek forms more than the original Hebrew name. For examples of the latter, see "Isaac" (Section 3.F), or "Solomon" (2.C).

A section containing Hebrew words occurring less than ten times was prepared for this project. Simply for considerations of length it has not been included in this volume. (It was twice as long as Sections 1-4, both in number of entries and estimated page length!) Most Hebrew students would probably find little use for this section of Hebrew vocabulary.

In the case of the Aramaic vocabulary (Section 6), the effort has been made to include every Aramaic word, except for proper nouns. (No personal or place names have been included, except for a few that occur more than fifty times in Aramaic *and* Hebrew and thus are listed in Sections 1-4 with a note regarding the number of occurrences in Aramaic.)

A glance at the Table of Contents and the first few vocabulary lists should be enough to clarify the arrangement of this volume. Instead of juggling two or three (or more) different frequency lists, all words of a given frequency range have been gathered into one list. By learning one list (or series of lists)— not two or three— a student can master all Hebrew (or Aramaic) words in that frequency range. Vocabulary learning effort can thus be better focused.

Furthermore, instead of setting arbitrary frequency ranges, this *Student's Vocabulary* has had as its priority the production of consistently short, manageable lists. In general, this means lists not in excess of thirty words. This ideal holds true until sheer numbers of words of identical frequency make smaller lists impossible, short of artificially breaking up longer lists alphabetically. (You can't have words that occur between 1.5 and 1.2 times in the MT!)

By these two devices then, combining all MT vocabulary into one sequence of lists containing less and less frequently-occurring words, and adjusting frequency ranges to keep lists reasonably short, this *Student's Vocabulary* has sought to meet the pedagogical shortcomings of other available Hebrew vocabularies.

Resources for the Preparation of *A Student's Vocabulary*

A number of reference works have been used in the determination of word frequencies. Trial lists were prepared based on frequencies given by Landes and Payne. However, all the words included in this vocabulary have been independently checked— except where the number of occurrences obviously exceed 5000— by an actual count. The primary reference works have been the concordances by Lisowsky and Mandelkern. Additionally, occasional reference has been made to Wigram's *Englishman's Hebrew and Chaldee Concordance*. Consult the Bibliography for publication details.

Acknowledgements

Without the help and encouragement of a large number of people this volume would not have been produced. In particular I think of two of my students at Pacific Union College, Larry Errett and Cathemae Cecchin. Larry Errett, an able linguist, did some of the earliest work on word counts, especially in the highest frequencies. And Cathe Cecchin, who worked as my

secretary for three years during her undergraduate study, has nearly single-handedly accomplished the staggering task of entering encoded text destined to be translated by computer into printed and pointed Hebrew script and (at the cost of even more effort) phonetic spellings.

W. Larry Richards, Religion Department chairman during the more critical stages of research for this volume, provided much-needed encouragement, but also the sorts of scheduling concessions without which this entire project might well have foundered. Small academic institutions seldom have adequate research-support resources. However, the administration of Pacific Union College has been most helpful and cooperative, supplying both the funds for student assistants and the resources and expertise of the College computer facility.

For computer aid and expertise, Harold E. Hunt and Bernard Maron of Autographics, Inc., in Monterey Park, California, richly deserve praise. It was their work that helped turn a concept into reality, and this even though all too often my idea of how to reach reality represented rather different ways of doing things. And here at Pacific Union College, our work of data entry was made immeasurably easier, and therefore more accurate and less time-consuming, by the efforts of Dr. Gilbert Muth, chairman of the Biology Department, a man who writes elegant computer programs that work (no mean feat!).

And finally, to my wife Carola, and to Carmie and Jason, I owe a large debt for constant support and understanding. Work on this project has consumed time that would have otherwise been theirs.

While every reasonable effort has been made to reduce errors to an absolute minimum, it is virtually certain a few such will remain. I would welcome any notices for corrections or improvements. Send these either directly to me or to the publisher.

Learning Hebrew vocabulary requires a lot of time and effort. I hope this volume will help both instructors and students of biblical Hebrew and Aramaic to make the most efficient use possible of their vocabulary study time.

Larry A. Mitchel
Pacific Union College
Angwin, California 94508
December 1983

HOW TO USE THIS *STUDENT'S VOCABULARY*

General Orientation

The purpose of vocabulary study is to learn the correct spelling, pronunciation, and meaning of a set of new (foreign or native) words. Since correct pronunciation of Hebrew words is an integral part of effective vocabulary learning, the student should from the beginning take seriously the matter of consonant and vowel values in Hebrew. For convenience a Table of Values has been provided for reference. However, these values will simply have to be committed to memory before efficient study of Hebrew vocabulary can begin.

Beyond the phonetic value of the Hebrew consonants and vowels themselves, Hebrew pronunciation is also determined by several other interrelated factors:

(1) Syllable division. Hebrew syllables may be either "open" (consisting of a consonant followed by a vowel) or "closed" (a consonant, a vowel, and a consonant— in that order). For the rules governing the use of long or short vowels (and non-vowels) in a Hebrew word, the student should consult his/her grammar. (The "half-open syllables" are discussed below under "Phonetic Spelling.")

(2) Use of *šəwâ*. Pronunciation of Hebrew words also depends upon a determination as to whether the "non-vowel" *šəwâ* is "vocal" (stands under the opening consonant of a syllable) or "silent" (under the closing consonant of a syllable).

(3) Accent. The placement of the stress in a Hebrew word can materially affect its pronunciation. This is especially obvious when the form of a word changes, for example in the formation of a plural or the addition of suffixes. In this vocabulary, accent marks are only used for multi-syllable Hebrew words that are stressed on other than the final syllable. The mark ` ˋ ` is used.

(4) Furtive *pátaḥ*. Some Hebrew words that end in guttural letters (especially ח and ע) must be treated uniquely in pronunciation. Though the final consonant has a *pátaḥ* under it, the vowel is pronounced *before* the consonant. Note that furtive *pátaḥ* is written in phonetic spelling as a raised *a* ([a]). The common practice, observed herein, is not to show a syllable division in phonetic spelling for furtive *pátaḥ*. Contrary to the practice of some grammars and lexicons, in this vocabulary the Hebrew forms show the accent mark. (Example: רָקִיעַ, rā/qî[a].)

Because of these and other variables, it was decided to include in this vocabulary a phonetic rendition (transliteration) of each form presented. In cases where more than one Semitic form is involved, transliterations are given in the same order as the Hebrew (or Aramaic) words. Syllable divisions and stress accents are also indicated.

Beyond proper spelling and pronunciation, the student needs to learn the meaning of the Hebrew words he/she is studying. The definitions that have been provided in this volume are basically correct, and have been chosen in consultation with standard Hebrew lexicons (particularly William L. Holladay's *A Concise Hebrew and Aramaic Lexicon of the Old Testament.*). These meanings are in no sense full and exhaustive. For the meanings of nouns in various contexts, or of verbs in different contexts or in derived conjugation stems, the student must consult a trustworthy dictionary or lexicon. See the Bibliography for a number of helpful and reliable lexicons and dictionaries. Individual language teachers may wish for whatever reason to supplement or emphasize (and even in some cases supplant) given definitions. But in general the meanings given for the Hebrew words in this vocabulary have been chosen with the beginning student in mind, and do provide base meanings that will serve those needs.

This *Student's Vocabulary* can be used to great advantage along with *A Reader's Hebrew-English Lexicon of the Old Testament* by Armstrong, Busby, and Carr. By simply learning the Hebrew vocabulary down to fifty occurrences, about 739 words in all, a student should be able to read plain Hebrew text by following along in the appropriate section of the *Reader's Lexicon,* and referring there for all forms which occur less than fifty times (assuming a minimum knowledge of grammar and syntax).

Sample Entry and Explanation

Perhaps the best way to explain how the individual vocabulary entries in this volume are presented is to give examples and provide some detailed explanations. The following entries are in no way complete and exhaustive, but what they do not contain can be easily described.

בָּקַשׁ[1] (Pi)[2] seek[3] [bā/qáš][4] 225[5]

(II)[6] אֵת (prep)[2] with, beside ['ēt] 5000[5]

[1] Hebrew/Aramaic Words. An attempt has been made to use forms and spellings that are favored today. In making such choices, personal judgments are inevitable. Not all decisions may seem to every trained reader to be the best ones. Hopefully no decision will mislead the beginning student. One such judgment relates to Hebrew and Aramaic words spelled with a long "o." In very many cases the word appears in the MT spelled with both "defective *ḥōlem*" (, ō) and with "full *ḥōlem*" (וֹ, ô). This vocabulary has not achieved consistency on the matter: if you can not find a word under one spelling, try the alternate spelling before giving up! (The same goes for full and defective spellings with— and without— *yōd*.)

a. Verbs: unpronounceable words are more difficult to to learn— at least if the ear helps at all in vocabulary study. For this reason all verb roots have been provided with vowels. In the case of verbs that only occur in non-*Qal* stems (and are thus left unpointed in most lexicons), this *Student's Vocabulary* gives to the root those vowels that pertain to the (missing) *Qal* form. Since this form is hypothetical, an asterisk (*) is placed after the entry. This practice has also been observed for the so-called hollow verbs (verbs with a *yōd* or *wāw* in the second position), even though the verb may in fact appear in just that form. (This has been done because there is often uncertainty, and some disagreement, regarding the appropriate vowel.) Furthermore, in many cases the verb, though used in the *Qal*, may not occur in the third masculine singular even though the asterisk is missing.

b. Nouns, adjectives, prepositions: an asterisk after these forms signals that while this is the dictionary form of the word, for one reason or another the word never appears just this way in the MT. (As a rule, simple changes in form, such as the addition of a suffixed pronoun or the construct state have not been listed in this vocabulary with an asterisk.) An explanation of the reason for the asterisk is provided in the definition section.

c. General comments: the names of ancient Near Eastern countries and their respective gentilic (people-naming) nouns have been combined in single entries, and listed according to total number of occurrences.

Numerals have also been gathered into single entries, corresponding words for multiples of ten ("twenty," "thirty," etc.) being given under the Hebrew word for that number. Numbers from three to ten are identified by the gender of the *form*. (In that range Hebrew uses feminine numerals for masculine nouns, and vice versa— a device called "chiastic concord" in some grammars).

Occasionally, particularly for words of low frequency, there is considerable uncertainty even regarding a hypothetical vowel-point assignment. In such cases the Semitic word is followed by a question mark in parentheses (?).

Defective *ḥōlem* can be located in a variety of places over a Hebrew word. The practice of placing this vowel point toward the left margin of wider Hebrew consonants has been followed herein, as well as the practice of not double-dotting *šîn* when it is preceeded by defective *ḥōlem*. Defective *ḥōlem* preceeding *ʾālep* is commonly written over the *right* margin of the latter, and has been written that way in this volume.

[2] Grammar/Morphology: information of importance or convenience about a word's part of speech, conjugation stem, or person/gender/number is given in abbreviated form preceding the definitions. The meaning of these abbreviations may be found in the list of Abbreviations and Symbols.

In the case of verbs that do not appear in the MT in the *Qal* stem, the Hebrew form appears in this vocabulary with an asterisk (as mentioned above). The note in parentheses at the beginning of the definition section then indicates the most commonly-used (or the simplest) derived-conjugation stem in which that verb does occur.

In the case of nouns, adjectives, prepositions, and such, the note in parentheses identifies the part of speech and/or the reason why the asterisk has been used.

[3] Word Meaning: levels of difference in the meanings for a given word have been indicated by separating punctuation marks: a comma divides words which are more or less synonymous, whereas a semicolon sets off extended meanings or rather different definitions. Roman numerals in parentheses refer to one of two or more roots with an identical spelling in Hebrew/Aramaic. These designations follow Holladay's lexicon. Definitions are of the Semitic word as given (not, for example, in plural, even if the asterisk means that this word only occurs in the plural form).

Cross references in the vocabulary are identified by Section number and Subsection letter (Example: Cf 1.D).

[4] Phonetic Spelling: as an aid to self-study, each entry includes a phonetic spelling. Beginning students should find this feature to be helpful as they begin to learn Semitic vocabulary, since it will aid in correct pronunciation of Hebrew/Aramaic words, thus enlisting the ear as well in vocabulary learning. It will be necessary to learn the proper values for each symbol from the Table of Values. Syllables are separated by slashes (/). Accented syllables have been indicated, except for mono-syllabic words.

"Half-open syllables" are neither open nor closed. Such syllables appear to defy syllable-formation rules in that they contain a short vowel, are unaccented, but stand without a closing consonant. Printed Hebrew Bibles commonly use a *méteḡ* to mark these syllables (a short verticle mark just to the left of the vowel point). Lexicons vary in their treatment of half-open syllables. In this volume those few such syllables are not marked in the Hebrew word. Rather, in the phonetic spelling the syllable is followed by an exclamation point (Example: מַעְרָכָה, ma!/ʾărā/ḵâ).

[5] Number of Occurrences: counts for Hebrew words are inclusive and for that reason somewhat overlapping. This means, for example, that a *Qal* active participle may be counted among the occurrences of the verb, and counted again when used as a noun. Such situations are limited primarily to words which occur often enough as substantives to justify also treating them as a vocabulary entry in their own right. In the case of *Qal* participles, only those occuring ten times or more have been listed in their own entries.

Commonly, word counts include forms of the word that have been prefixed (by the article or prepositions), pluralized, and/or suffixed (by pronouns). In some situations in which such forms have become standardized (and are numerous), prefixed or suffixed forms are listed in separate entries. For verbs, the indicated count includes not only the implied or indicated verbal stems (*Qal, Hip̄ʿil*, etc.), but all stems in which that verb appears.

Word counts from Lisowsky's concordance include *Qərê* readings as well as normal occurrences. With proper nouns (where given), all occurrences of a given name are included, even though in many cases more than one referent is intended.

In cases where Mandelkern and Lisowsky disagree as to number of occurrences, the general practice has been to enter the higher of the counts, unless further work (sometimes including entry-by-entry comparisons) has made it clear the lower number is to be preferred.

Words identified as occurring 5000 times occur *more* than 5000 times; no attempt has been made to precisely establish the occurrences of these twelve Hebrew words.

[6] Root Number: as indicated earlier, root designations follow Holladay's lexicon. In some cases several roots have been combined, for one reason or another, into one entry. In such situations the meanings of the various roots have been designated within the definition section.

Suggestions for Using this *Student's Vocabulary*

As has been widely acknowledged, learning vocabulary and retaining it are probably the most challenging aspects of learning Hebrew or Aramaic. In my experience the principal reason for this fact is that, in contrast to New Testament Greek, Old Testament Hebrew and Aramaic have virtually no cognate words in English. This requires much more rote memorization, or the formation of idiosyncratic memory devices. While each student must determine what works best for vocabulary study, here are a few common sense suggestions:

(1) Flash cards. While not all language students use them, home-made flash cards provide several advantages in vocabulary learning. First, you must go through the motions of writing the foreign word and its definition. Second, punched and carded on a ring holder, flash cards are very transportable for study at odd times and in many places. Third, flash cards can be (and probably should be) rearranged as you learn words, so that less time is spent on words that only need to be reviewed while more effort is concentrated on new or recalcitrant forms.

(2) Oral repetition. Repeating Hebrew and Aramaic words and their meanings out loud over and over (correctly!) introduces two critical factors into your vocabulary learning— pronunciation and hearing.

(3) Repeated writing. Used alone and in connection with oral repetition, repeated writing of OT vocabulary helps to establish a memory pattern.

Given the descending-frequency scheme with which this volume is prepared, a student can develop a Hebrew or Aramaic vocabulary as far as is necessary or desired (within the limits of this vocabulary volume). Within the ranges covered herein, by using the Index and referring to the appropriate Section/ Subsection location, the number of times a given word occurs in the OT can be determined.

BIBLIOGRAPHY

Armstrong, Terry A.; Busby, Douglas S.; and Carr, Cyril F. *A Reader's Hebrew-English Lexicon of the Old Testament*. Vol. I: Genesis-Deuteronomy. Grand Rapids: Zondervan, 1980.
_____. Vol, II: Joshua - 2 Kings (1982).
_____. Vol. III: Announced.
Brown, Francis; Driver, S. R.; and Briggs, Charles A. *A Hebrew and English Lexicon of the Old Testament*. Oxford: Clarendon Press, 1907.
Cohen, Harold R. (Chaim). *Biblical Hapax Legomena in the Light of Akkadian and Ugaritic*. SBL Dissertation Series, 37. Missoula: Scholars Press, 1978.
Feyerabend, Karl. *Langenscheidt's Pocket Hebrew Dictionary to the Old Testament*. New York: Barnes & Noble, 1961.
Fohrer, Georg. *Hebrew and Aramaic Dictionary of the Old Testament*. Trans. by W. Johnstone. Berlin: Walter de Gryter, 1971.
Holladay, William L. *A Concise Hebrew and Aramaic Lexicon of the Old Testament*. Grand Rapids: Eerdmans, 1971; sixth impression, January 1982.
Koehler, Ludwig and Baumgartner, Walter, editors. *Lexicon in Veteris Testamenti Libros*. One volume with Supplement. Leiden: Brill, 1958.
_____. *Hebräisches und aramäisches Lexicon zum alten Testament*. Third edition. Parts I and II. Leiden: Brill, 1967, 1974.
Lambdin, Thomas. *Introduction to Biblical Hebrew*. New York: Scribner's, 1971.
Landes, George M. *A Student's Vocabulary of Biblical Hebrew. Listed According to Frequency and Cognate*. New York: Scribner's, 1961.
Lisowsky, Gerhard. *Konkordanz zum Hebräischen alten Testament*. Second edition. Stuttgart: Deutsche Bibelgesellschaft, 1958.
Mandelkern, Solomon. *Veteris Testamenti Concordantiae Hebraicae atque Chaldaicae*. Third edition. Jerusalem: Schocken, 1967.
_____. *Veteris Testamenti Concordantiae Hebraicae atque Chaldaicae*. Seventh edition, augmented and revised by F. Margolin and M. Gottstein. Jerusalem: Shocken, 1967.
Payne, J. Barton. *Hebrew Vocabularies. Based on Harper's Hebrew Vocabularies*. Grand Rapids: Baker, 1956.
Watts, John D. W. *Lists of Words Occurring Frequently in the Hebrew Bible*. Second edition. Leiden: Brill, 1967

Wigram, George V. *The Englishman's Hebrew and Chaldee Concordance of the Old Testament*. Fourth edition. London: Samuel Bagster & Sons, 1843.

Young, Robert. *Analytical Concordance to the Bible*. New York: Funk & Wagnalls, n.d.

TABLE OF VALUES

NOTE: Protocols adopted here are essentially those of Thomas Lambdin (*Introduction to Biblical Hebrew*. New York: Scribner's, 1971; pages XXII-XXIII.) See also G. Johannes Botterweck and Helmer Ringgren, eds. *Theological Dictionary of the Old Testament*. Vol. I. Grand Rapids: Eerdmans, 1974; page XX.

Symbol (Name)	Transliteration Value	Pronunciation Guidelines
Consonants		
א (*ʾālep̄*)	ʾ	(glottal stop—none)
ב (*bêt*)	b	*b* as in "best"
ב	b̠	*v* as in "vest"
ג (*gîmel*)	g	*g* as in "give"
ג	ḡ	throaty *gh*
ד (*dālet*)	d	*d* as in "day"
ד	d̠	*th* as in "the one"
ה (*hē*)	h	*h* as in "hay"
ו (*wāw*)	w	*w* as in "well"
ז (*záyin*)	z	*z* as in "zero"
ח (*ḥēt*)	ḥ	*ch* as in Scots *loch* or German *buch*
ט (*ṭēt*)	ṭ	*t* as in "time"
י (*yōd̠*)	y	*y* as in "yes"
כ (*kap̄*)	k	*k* as in "key"
כ	k̠	*ch* as in German Bach
ך (final form)	k̠	*ch* as in German Bach
ל (*lāmed̠*)	l	*l* as in "look"
מ (*mēm*)	m	*m* as in "more"
ם (final form)	m	*m* as in "more"
נ (*nûn*)	n	*n* as in "now"
ן (final form)	n	*n* as in "now"
ס (*sāmek̠*)	s	*s* as in "say"
ע (*ʿáyin*)	ʿ	(glottal stop—none)
פ (*pēh*)	p	*p* as in "pay"

פ	p̄	*f* as in "face"
ף (final form)	p̄	*f* as in "face"
צ (*ṣaḏēh*)	ṣ	*ts* as in "sits"
ץ (final form)	ṣ	*ts* as in "sits"
ק (*qōp̄*)	q	harder than *c* in "cool"
ר (*rēš*)	r	*r* as in "ran"
שׂ (*śîn*)	ś	*s* as in "say"
שׁ (*šîn*)	š	*sh* as in "show"
ת (*tāw*)	t	*t* as in "try"
ת	t̲	*th* as in "thin "

Vowels and Diphthongs

הָ	â	*a* as in "father"
י (*ḥîreq-yōḏ*)	î	*i* as in "machine"
י (*ṣĕrê-yōḏ*)	ê	*ey* as in "they"
וֹ (full *ḥōlem*)	ô	*o* as in "note"
(defective *ḥōlem*)	ō	*o* as in "note"
וּ (*šûreq*)	û	*u* as in "flute"
ָ (*qāmeṣ*)	ā	*a* as in "father"
ֵ (*ṣĕrê*)	ē	*ey* as in "they"
ִ (*ḥîreq*)	i	*i* as in "pin"
ֶ (*səḡōl*)	e	*e* as in "let"
ַ (*páṯaḥ*)	a	*a* as in "that"
ָ (*qāmeṣ-ḥāṭûp̄*)	o	*o* as in "top"
ֻ (*qibbûṣ*)	u	*u* as in "bull"
ַ (furtive *páṯaḥ*)	raised ᵃ	*a* as in "account"
ְ (simple *šəwâ*)	ə	*a* as in "about"
ֲ (*ḥāṭēp̄-páṯaḥ*)	ă	*a* as in "about"
ֱ (*ḥāṭēp̄-səḡōl*)	ĕ	*a* as in "about"
ֳ (*ḥāṭēp̄-qāmeṣ*)	ŏ	*a* as in "about"
יַ	ai	*ay* as in "say"
יָ	āi	*i* as in "sigh"
יֶ	ey	*ey* as in "they"
וֹי, יֹ	ôy, ōy	*oy* as in "toy"
וּי	ûy	*uey* as in "gluey"
וָ	āw	*ow* as in "how"
וַ	aw	*ow* as in "prow"
יו	îw	*ue* as in "hue"
וֵ, יו	ēw, êw	*av* as in "save"

ABBREVIATIONS AND SYMBOLS

abs	absolute	Hithpal	*Hiṯpalpel*
act	active	Hithpol	*Hiṯpoʿlel*
adj	adjective	Ho	*Hop̄ʿal*
adv	adverb	idiom	idiom; idiomatic
advs	adversative (conjunction)		expression
alw	always	imprec	imprecative
c	common (gender)	impv	imperative
cf	compare, see also; see	inf	infinitive
	instead	interj	interjection
cj	conjecture; conjectural	interr	interrogative
coll	collective	intrans	intransitive
comp	comparison; comparative	irr	irregular
conj	conjunction	K	*Kəṯib* (what is written in
cons	consonant		MT)
cstr	construct	m	masculine
ctxt	context(ual); in context	MT	Masoretic Text
def	definite	met	metaphor(ically)
dem	demonstrative	n	noun
den	denominative	neg	negative
ditt	dittography	Ni	*Nip̄ʿal*
du	dual	ord	ordinal (number)
emph	emphatic (Aramaic)	Pa	*Paʿel* (Aramaic)
ext	by extension; extended	part	participle
	meaning	pass	passive
f	feminine	pers	person(al)
fract	fractional (number)	Pe	*Peʿal* (Aramaic)
gent	gentilic (noun)	Pi	*Piʿel*
Ha	*Hap̄ʿel* (Aramaic)	Pil	*Piʿlel*
Hi	*Hip̄ʿil*	Pilp	*Pilpel*
Hisht	*Hištap̄ʿel*	pl	plural
Hith	*Hiṯpaʿel* (Hebrew);	Po	*Poʿel*
	Hiṯpeʿel (Aramaic)	poet	poetic; in poetry
Hithpa	*Hiṯpaʿal* (Aramaic)	Pol	*Poʿlel, Poʿlal*

poss	possible	*	hypothethical form (as such does not occur in MT)
pr	pronoun		
pred	predicate		
pref	prefix(ed)	!	indicates half-open syllable
prep	preposition		
prob	probable	?	indicates uncertainty regarding definition
Pul	*Puʿlal*		
Q	*Qərê* (what should be read in MT)	(?)	indicates uncertainty regarding Semitic vowel(s)
rel	relative		
s	singular	†	indicates Aramaic cognate spelled like a Hebrew word
stat	stative		
trad	traditional(ly)		
trans	transitive	‡	indicates Aramaic cognate with different *vowels* from Hebrew
txt corr	text(ual) corrupt(ion)		
unc	uncertain		
unex	unexplained	§	indicates Aramaic cognate spelled *differently* but *recognizably*
v	verb		
voc	vocative		
wp	word play		

SECTION 1: HEBREW WORDS OCCURRING MORE THAN 500 TIMES (106)

A. *Words Occurring More Than 2200 Times (25)*

אֶל (prep) unto, toward [ʾel] 5000

(II) אֱלֹהִים God [ʾĕlō/hīm] 2706

(I) אָמַר say [ʾā/már] 5000

אֶרֶץ earth [ʾé/reṣ] 2498

אֲשֶׁר (rel pr) who, which, that [ʾăšér] 5000

(I) אֵת (accusative particle; definite object marker; not translated) [ʾēṯ] 5000

(II) אֵת (prep) with, beside [ʾēṯ] 5000

בְּ- (pref prep) in 5000

בּוֹא go in, enter, come [bôʾ] 2530

(I) בֵּן son [bēn] 4887

הַ- (pref def art) the (with *dāḡēš* in following cons) 5000

הֲ- (pref interr particle) 5000

הָיָה be, happen, become [hā/yâ] 3514

וְ- (pref conj) and, also, even 5000

יהוה; יָה, יָה (full; short form) The Lord [K "Yahweh" ?; Qʾ ădō/nái; yâ] 5766

(I) יוֹם day [yôm] 2241

יִשְׂרָאֵל Israel [yiś/rā/ʾēl] 2513

כְּ- (pref prep) as, like 5000

(II) כִּי (conj) because, for, that, when, but; indeed, truly [kî] 4395

כֹּל, כּוֹל all, every [kōl, kôl] 5000

לְ- (pref prep) to, toward (I); (voc) Do! Yes! (II) 5000

לֹא (neg) no, not [lōʾ] 4973

(I) מֶלֶךְ king [mé/lek] 2522

(II) עַל (prep) on, upon, against, over [ʿal] 4898

עָשָׂה do, make; (Pi) press, squeeze (II?) [ʾā/śâ] 2573

B. *Words Occurring between 2199 and 1000 Times (27)*

אָב father [ʾāḇ] 1568

(I) אִישׁ; אֲנָשִׁים (s; pl) man [ʾîš; ʾănā/šīm] 2149

אִם (conj) if, then [ʾim] 1046

אֲנִי; אָנֹכִי (pers pr c) I [ʾănî; ʾā/nō/kî] 1316

(I) בַּיִת house [bá/yit] 2039

(II) דָּבַר* (Pi) speak [dā/ḇár*] 1130

דָּבָר word, thing, matter [dā/b̲ár] 1426

דָּוִד David [dā/wíd̲] 1031

הוּא (pers pr) he [hû'] 1533

הָלַךְ go, walk [hā/lák̲] 1504

הֵמָּה; הֵנָּה (pers pr pl m; f) they [hḗm/mâ; hḗn/nâ] 1553

הִנֵּה (dem interj) behold! lo! (cf I הֵן, 3.G) [hin/néh] 1037

זֶה; זֹאת (dem pr, s m; f) this [zeh; zō'ṯ] 1752

יָד hand [yād̲] 1580

יָצָא go (come) out, go (come) forth [yā/ṣā'] 1055

יָשַׁב sit, dwell, inhabit [yā/šáb̲] 1078

לִפְנֵי (prep) before [lip̲/nê] 1099

מִן (prep) from, out of, part of, because of; (comp) than [min] 1279

נָתַן give [nā/ṯán] 1994

(II) עַד (prep) to, unto, as far as (spacial); until, while (temporal) ['ad̲] 1246

(I) עִיר; עָרִים (f; irr pl) city ['îr; 'ā/rím̲] 1080

(II) עַם people ['am] 1827

עִם (prep) with ['im] 1076

פָּנִים face [pā/ním̲] 2120

רָאָה see [rā/'â] 1294

שׁוּב turn, return [šûb̲] 1055

שָׁמַע hear, give ear to, obey [šā/má'] 1136

C. Words Occurring from 999 Times to 730 Times (28)

אָדוֹן; אֲדֹנָי lord, master; the Lord ['ā/d̲ṓn; 'ăd̲ō/nái] 770

אֶחָד; אַחַת (s m; f) one ['e/ḥád̲; 'a!/ḥáṯ] 959

(I) אַיִן; אֵין (abs; cstr) there is/are not (non-existence) ['á/yin; 'ên] 773

אָכַל eat, devour ['ā/k̲ál] 795

(I) אַל no, not ['al] 738

אֵלֶּה (dem pr; c pl) these ['ḗl/leh] 738

אִשָּׁה; נָשִׁים (s; irr pl) woman ['iš/šâ; nā/ším̲] 779

אַתָּה; אַתְּ (s m; f) you ['at/tấ; 'at] 893

גַּם (adv, conj) also, indeed [gam] 812

יָדַע know, notice [yā/d̲á'] 924

(I) יְהוּדָה; יְהוּדִי Judah; (gent adj, n) Judean, Judahite [yəhû/d̲ấ; yəhû/d̲î] 889

כֹּהֵן priest [kō/hḗn] 749

לֵב; לֵבָב heart [lēb̲; lē/b̲áb̲] 844

לָקַח take [lā/qáḥ] 964

מָה, מֶה, מַה (interr pr) what? how? [mâ, meh, mah] 760

מוּת die [mûṯ] 737

מֹשֶׁה Moses [mō/šéh] 763

נֶפֶשׁ life, self; throat [né/p̲eš] 753

(I) עֶבֶד servant ['é/b̲ed̲] 800

עַיִן eye; fountain ['á/yin] 867

עָלָה go up ['ā/lấ] 879

עָשָׂר; עֶשְׂרִים (s m; c pl) ten (plus num. = 11-19); twenty [ʿǎ/śǎr; ʿeś/rîm] 819

קָרָא (I) call, meet; read (aloud) [qā/rǎʾ] 730

שָׁלַח stretch out, let go, send [šā/lǎḥ] 839

שָׁם (adv) there [šām] 817

שֵׁם (I) name [šēm] 862

שָׁנָה year [šā/nâ] 871

שְׁנַיִם; שְׁתַּיִם (du m; f) two [šǝná/yim; šǝtá/yim] 739

D. Words Occurring between 729 and 500 Times (26)

אָדָם (I) man [ʾā/ḏǎm] 553

אָח (II) brother [ʾāḥ] 626

אַחַר behind, after [ʾaǃ/ḥǎr] 713

בַּת (I) daughter [baṯ] 582

גָּדוֹל (adj) great [gā/ḏôl] 525

גּוֹי people, nation [gôy] 545

דֶּרֶךְ way, road, journey; (ext) custom [dé/reḵ] 698

הִיא (pers pr) she [hîʾ] 541

הַר mountain, range [har] 554

טוֹב (I) (v) be good; (adj) good; (n) goodness [ṭôḇ] 612

יְרוּשָׁלַם (Q) Jerusalem (26 times in Aramaic) [yǝrû/šā/lá/im] 667

כַּאֲשֶׁר (conj) as [kaǃ/ʾǎšér] 504

כֹּה (adv) thus, so [kōh] 554

כֵּן (adv, adj, n) rightly, upright, right (I); (adv) thus, so (II) [kēn] 707

מֵאָה (I) hundred; (du) two hundred [mē/ʾā] 577

מַיִם water [má/yim] 574

מִצְרַיִם; מִצְרִי Egypt; (gent) Egyptian [miṣ/rá/yim; miṣ/rî] 708

נָכָה* (Ni) be hit; (Hi) smite [nā/kâ*] 504

נָשָׂא lift up, bear, carry [nā/śǎʾ] 651

עָבַר (I) pass over, transgress [ʿā/ḇǎr] 539

עָמַד stand [ʿā/mǎḏ] 519

קוּם* rise, stand [qûm*] 624

רֹאשׁ (I) head [rōʾš] 593

רַע, רַע; רָעָה (s m; f; adj, n) evil [rāʿ, raʿ; rā/ʿâ] 661

שִׂים* (I) set, place [śîm*] 584

שָׁלֹשׁ, שְׁלֹשָׁה; שְׁלֹשִׁים (s m, f; pl) three; thirty [šā/lóš, šǝlō/šâ; šǝlō/šîm] 586

SECTION 2: HEBREW WORDS OCCURRING BETWEEN 500 AND 200 TIMES (136)

A. *Words Occurring between 500 and 400 Times (28)*

אֶ֫לֶף thousand (II?); tribe, clan (III?) [ˈé/leₚ] 494

אַרְבַּע, אַרְבָּעָה; (I) אַרְבָּעִים (s m, f; pl) four; forty [ˈar/báˈ, ˈar/- bā/ˈấ; ˈar/bā/ˈîm] 444

בְּתוֹךְ Cf תָּ֫וֶךְ

חָמֵשׁ, חֲמִשָּׁה; חֲמִשִּׁים (s m, f; pl) five; fifty [ḥā/méš, ḥămiš/šấ; ḥămiš/šîm] 478

חֶ֫רֶב sword [ḥé/reḇ] 407

יָלַד bring forth, bear [yā/láḏ] 488

מִזְבֵּ֫חַ altar [miz/béaḥ] 401

מִי (interr) who? [mî] 406

מָצָא find; (Hi) present [mā/ṣáˈ] 451

מִשְׁפָּט judgment, custom, justice [miš/páṭ] 425

(I) נָא (particle of entreaty) pray, now; please [nāˈ] 401

נָפַל fall [nā/p̄ál] 433

עוֹד yet, still, again [ˈôḏ] 481

עוֹלָם, עֹלָם remote time; forever, eternity [ˈô/lắm; ˈō/lắm] 434

עַתָּה now [ˈat/tấ] 432

פֶּה; כְּפִי, לְפִי mouth; (conj) according to [peh; kəp̄î, ləp̄î] 492

(I) צָבָא service in war; host, army [ṣā/ḇấ] 485

צָוָה* (Pi) command [ṣā/- wấ*] 494

קֹ֫דֶשׁ (adj, n) holy (thing) [qṓ/ḏeš] 430

קוֹל voice, sound [qôl] 499

רַב (adj) much, many (I?); (ctxt) captain, chief (II?) [raḇ] 475

שַׂר official, leader, prince [śar] 412

שָׁאוּל Saul [šā/ˈûl] 406

שֶׁ֫בַע, שִׁבְעָה; (I) שִׁבְעִים (s m, f; pl) seven; seventy [šé/ḇaˈ, šiḇ/ˈấ; šiḇ/ˈîm] 492

שָׁמַ֫יִם heavens, sky [šā/má/yim] 416

שָׁמַר keep watch, guard [šā/már] 465

תָּ֫וֶךְ; בְּתוֹךְ midst, middle; (prep) within, through [tắ/weḵ; bətôḵ] 416

(I) תַּ֫חַת (prep) beneath, under, instead of [tá/ḥat] 490

B. *Words Occurring 399 through 310 Times (29)*

(I) אֹ֫הֶל tent [ˈṓ/hel] 342

אַהֲרֹן Aaron [ˈa!/hărṓn] 347

אוֹ (conj) or [ˈô] 311

(I) אֵשׁ fire [ˈēš] 375

אַתֶּם; אַתֵּן (pl m; f) you ['at/tém; 'at/tén] 330

בֵּין; בַּיִן (cstr prep) between; (n) interval [bên; bá/-yin] 396

בָּנָה build [bā/nấ] 373

(II) בָּרַךְ bless [bā/rák] 328

דָּם blood [dām] 356

זָהָב gold [zā/háb] 383

חַי; חַיִּים (n) life (I), (adj) living (II); (pl) lifetime (I) [ḥai; ḥay/yîm] 386

יָם sea; (ext) west [yām] 392

יַעֲקֹב Jacob [ya!/'ăqób] 348

(I) יָרֵא (stat) fear, be afraid [yā/ré'] 377

יָרַד go down [yā/rád] 380

כְּלִי vessel, utensil [kəlî] 324

כֶּסֶף silver [ké/seṗ] 399

לֵוִי Levi (4 times in Aramaic) [lē/wî] 353

מִלְחָמָה war, battle [mil/ḥā/-mấ] 319

(I) מָלַךְ reign, be king [mā/lák] 347

מָקוֹם place [mā/qốm] 399

נְאֻם utterance, declaration [nə'úm] 378

נָבִיא prophet [nā/bî'] 313

נָגַד (Hi) make known, report, tell [nā/ḡád] 369

(I) עָנָה answer ['ā/nấ] 314

עֵץ (also coll) tree ['ēṣ] 330

רוּחַ spirit, wind [rûªḥ] 376

שָׂדֶה; שָׂדַי open field [śā/déh; śā/dái] 332

(I) שַׁעַר gate [šá/'ar] 368

C. Words Occurring 309 through 270 Times (26)

אֹיֵב, אוֹיֵב enemy ['ō/yéb; 'ô/yéb] 281

(II) אַף nose, nostril; (ext) anger ['aṗ] 279

בָּבֶל; בַּבְלִי Babylon (Babel); (gent) Babylonians [bā/bél; bab/lái] 288

בְּרִית covenant [bərît] 287

בָּשָׂר flesh [bā/śár] 270

(I) חֹדֶשׁ new moon, month [ḥó/deš] 278

חָזַק be(come) strong; (Hi) seize, grasp [ḥā/záq] 288

חַטָּאת sin, sin-offering, expiation [ḥaṭ/ṭá't] 296

חָיָה live, be (stay) alive [ḥā/yấ] 281

כָּרַת cut off, fell, exterminate; make (a covenant) [kā/rát] 287

לֶחֶם bread [lé/ḥem] 296

מְאֹד (n) force, might; (adv) very, exceedingly [mə'ōd] 287

(I) מִדְבָּר pasturage, wilderness, steppe [mid/bár] 271

מִשְׁפָּחָה (extended) family; clan [miš/pā/ḥấ] 300

סָבִיב (n) circuit; (adv) all around, round about, surrounding [sā/bîb] 309

סוּר turn aside; (Hi) take away, remove [sûr] 298

עָבַד serve [ʿā/ḇáḏ] 289

(I) עֹלָה burnt offering [ʿō/lấ] 288

עֵת time [ʿēṯ] 282

פְּלִשְׁתִּי ;פְּלֶשֶׁת (gent n) Philistine(s); Philistia [pəliš/tî; pəlé/šeṯ] 294

פָּקַד visit, number, appoint; miss; take care of; muster [pā/qáḏ] 301

פַּרְעֹה Pharaoh [par/ʿóh] 273

צֹאן ;צֹנֶה flock [ṣōʾn; ṣō/néh] 275

קָרַב draw near [qā/ráḇ] 291

שְׁלֹמֹה Solomon [šəlō/móh] 293

שֵׁשׁ, שִׁשָּׁה; (s m, f; pl) six; sixty

(I) שִׁשִּׁים [šēš, šiš/šấ; ši/šîm] 272

D. Words Occurring 269 through 220 Times (31)

אֶבֶן (f) stone [ʾé/ḇen] 268

אַבְרָהָם ;אַבְרָם Abraham; Abram [ʾaḇ/rā/hám; ʾaḇ/rắm] 235

(I) אֲדָמָה ground [ʾăḏā/mấ] 225

(V) אֵל Mighty One, God (god) [ʾēl] 236

(I) אַמָּה forearm, cubit [ʾam/mấ] 226

בָּקַשׁ* (Pi) seek [bā/qáš*] 225

גְּבוּל boundary, territory [gəḇûl] 241

זָכַר remember [zā/ḵár] 230

זֶרַע seed [zé/raʿ] 228

חָטָא miss (a mark), sin [ḥā/ṭấ] 237

חַיִל strength; wealth; army [ḥá/yil] 246

(II) חֶסֶד loyalty, kindness, devotion, steadfast love [ḥé/seḏ] 250

יְהוֹשׁוּעַ ;יֵשׁוּעַ Joshua [yəhô/šûʿᵃ; yē/šûʿᵃ] 247

יָרַשׁ subdue, possess, dispossess (I?); tread (II?) [yā/ráš] 231

יָשַׁב (Qal part) inhabitant [yō/šéḇ] 260

כָּתַב write [kā/ṯáḇ] 222

לַיְלָה; לֵיל (m) night [lá/yəlâ; lá/-yil] 231

לְמַעַן (prep) for the sake of, on account of; (conj) in order that [ləmá/ʿan] 269

מוֹעֵד appointed place or time; season [mô/ʿéḏ] 223

מַטֶּה rod, staff; (ext) tribe [maṭ/ṭéh] 252

מָלֵא (stat) be full; (Pi) fill, fulfill [mā/lḗ] 250

מַעֲשֶׂה work [ma!/ʿăśéh] 235

(I) נַחֲלָה inheritance [na!/ḥălấ] 223

נַעַר lad, youth [ná/ʿar] 240

עָוֹן transgression, iniquity [ʿā/wón] 231

קֶרֶב; בְּקֶרֶב inward part, midst; (prep) in (the midst of) [qé/reḇ; bəqé/-reḇ] 227

(I) רָבָה be(come) numerous, be great; (Hi) multiply, make many [rā/ḇấ] 226

רֶגֶל foot [ré/ḡel] 252

רָשַׁע; רִשְׁעָה (s m;f; adj) guilty; (n) wicked (one) [rā/šáʿ; rəšā/ʿấ] 264

שָׁלוֹם peace, health [šā/lốm] 242

תּוֹרָה teaching, law [tô/rấ] 220

E. *Words Occurring 219 through 200 Times (22)*

אָהַב love, like [ʾā/háḇ] 205

אֵם mother [ʾēm] 219

אָסַף gather, take in [ʾā/sáp̄] 203

אֲרוֹן ark, chest [ʾărốn] 202

(II) בֶּגֶד garment [bé/ḡed] 214

(II) בֹּקֶר morning [bố/qer] 200

יוֹסֵף Joseph [yô/sḗp̄] 214

יָסַף add [yā/sáp̄] 212

יָשַׁע (Ni) be saved; (Hi) save [yā/šáʿ] 205

כָּבוֹד possessions, honor, glory [kā/ḇốd] 200

כּוּן (Ni) be firm, established; (Pol) establish; (Hi) prepare [kûn] 219

(I) כָּלָה cease, come to an end, finish, complete [kā/lấ] 204

מַחֲנֶה camp, army [ma!/ḥănéh] 219

מַלְאָךְ messenger [mal/ʾáḵ] 213

מִנְחָה gift; offering [min/ḥấ] 211

נָטָה turn, stretch out [nā/ṭấ] 215

נָצַל (Ni) be delivered; (Hi) snatch away [nā/ṣál] 208

(I) עָזַב leave, abandon [ʿā/záḇ] 212

צַדִּיק (adj) righteous, just [ṣad/dîq] 206

שָׁכַב lie down; have sexual intercourse [šā/káḇ] 211

שָׁפַט judge, enter into controversy; (Ni) plead [šā/p̄áṭ] 203

(II) שָׁתָה (v) drink [šā/ṭấ] 217

SECTION 3: HEBREW WORDS OCCURRING FROM 199 THROUGH 100 TIMES (185)

A. Words Occurring 199 through 175 Times (24)

אָבַד perish; (Pi) destroy; (Hi) exterminate [ʾā/ḇáḏ] 183

אֹ֫זֶן ear [ʾṓ/zen] 187

אֶפְרַ֫יִם; אֶפְרָתִי Ephraim; (gent) Ephraimite [ʾep̄/rá/yim; ʾep̄/rā/tî] 182

בְּהֵמָה; בְּהֵמוֹת cattle, animals; (pl of ext) crocodile? [bəhē/mã́; bəhē/mṓt] 192

בִּנְיָמִן; בֶּן־יְמִינִי Benjamin; (gent) Benjamites [bin/yā/mín; ben-yəmî/nî] 180

(I) בַּ֫עַל owner, husband; Baʿal [bá/ʿal] 198

בָּקָר (coll) cows, herd(s), cattle [bā/qár] 183

גָּלָה reveal, uncover (I?); depart, go into captivity (II?) [gā/lã́] 187

זָקֵן (adj) old; (n) old man, elder [zā/qḗn] 178

חָצֵר permanent settlement, court, enclosure [ḥā/ṣḗr] 193

יָכֹל (stat) be able [yā/ḵól] 194

יַרְדֵּן Jordan [yar/dḗn] 181

כַּף hand, palm [kap̄] 192

לָכֵן (adv) therefore [lā/kḗn] 196

מוֹאָב; מוֹאָבִי Moab; (gent) Moabite(s) [mô/ʾáḇ; mô/ʾā/ḇî] 199

מִצְוָה commandment [miṣ/wã́] 181

סֵ֫פֶר scroll [sḗ/p̄er] 185

רִאשׁוֹן (ord) first [riʾ/šṓn] 182

רוּם* be(come) high, exalted [rûm*] 195

(II) רֵ֫עַ friend, fellow, companion [rḗaʿ] 195

שָׂפָה lip; (ext) shore [śā/p̄ã́] 178

שֵׁ֫בֶט rod, staff; (ext) tribe [šḗ/ḇeṭ] 190

שָׁבַע* (Ni, Hi) swear [šā/ḇáʿ*] 186

שֶׁ֫מֶן oil [šḗ/men] 193

B. Words Occurring 174 through 160 Times (27)

(I) אַחֵר (adj) another [ʾa!/ḥḗr] 166

(I) אַ֫יִל ram [ʾá/yil] 161

אַךְ (adv) only; surely [ʾak] 160

(I) בָּחַר choose [bā/ḥár] 173

בִּין* understand, perceive [bîn*] 171

גִּבּוֹר warrior, mighty man [gib/bôr] 161

(II) דּוֹר generation, lifetime, life-span [dôr] 169

דָּרַשׁ seek [dā/ráš] 163

הָרַג kill [hā/ráḡ] 168

(I) זֶבַח (n) sacrifice [zé/baḥ] 162

(II) חָוָה* (Hisht) bow down [ḥā/wâ*] 174

חוּץ (n) place outside the house, street; (prep, adv) outside, without [ḥûṣ] 165

טָמֵא (stat) be unclean [ṭā/mḗ'] 161

כְּנַעַן; כְּנַעֲנִי Canaan; (gent) Canaanite [kəná/'an; kəna!/'ănî] 163

(I) לָחַם (Ni) fight [lā/ḥám] 171

לָמָּה, לָמָה (interr pr) why? [lắm/mâ, lā/mấ] 173

מְלָאכָה work [məlā'/ḵâ] 167

נוּס* flee [nûs*] 160

סָבַב turn around [sā/báḇ] 162

סָפַר write, count, number; (Pi) recount, report, enumerate [sā/p̄ár] 162

עֶשֶׂר ; עֲשָׂרָה (group of) ten, decade ['é/śer; 'ă/śārâ] 173

פֶּתַח gate, opening, entrance [pé/taḥ] 163

קָדַשׁ be holy; (Pi) consecrate [qā/dáš] 172

(I) רָעָה feed, graze, tend (cattle) [rā/'â] 171

שָׁאַל ask (for), demand [šā/'ál] 173

שָׁחָה see (II) חָוָה* 174

שָׁחַת* (Ni) be corrupt, spoiled; (Pi) spoil, ruin; (Hi) destroy [šā/ḥát*] 161

C. Words Occurring 159 through 144 Times (26)

אֲנַחְנוּ (pers pr c) we ['ănáḥ/nû] 156

אֲרָם; אֲרַמִּי Aram, Syria; (gent) Aramean(s), Syrian(s) ['ărám; 'ăram/mî] 155

אַשּׁוּר Assyria, (as gent) Assyrian ['aš/šûr] 152

(II) הָלַל* (Pi) praise; (Hith) boast [hā/lál*] 145

חָכְמָה experience, shrewdness, wisdom [ḥok/mâ] 152

יוֹאָב Joab [yô/'áḇ] 146

יִרְמְיָה; יִרְמְיָהוּ Jeremiah [yir/məyấ; yir/məyắ/hû] 147

כָּסָה* (Pi) cover, conceal [kā/sâ*] 157

לְבַד (adv) alone; (prep) besides [ləḇad] 155

מָוֶת death [mắ/weṯ] 159

מְנַשֶּׁה Manasseh [mənaš/šéh] 150

נֶגֶד (n, prep, adv) opposite, before [né/ḡeḏ] 151

נָגַע touch, reach; come to [nā/ḡá'] 150

נָסַע depart [nā/sáʿ] 146

(I) עֵדָה congregation [ʿē/ḏấ] 149

פַּר; פָּרָה (m; f) young bull; cow [par; pā/râ] 159

(I) פָּתַח open; (Pi) loosen, free [pā/ṭáḥ] 144

צְדָקָה righteousness [ṣəḏā/qấ] 157

צִיּוֹן Zion [ṣiy/yôn] 154

(I) צָפוֹן north [ṣā/p̄ôn] 153

רֹב multitude, abundance [rōḇ] 153

שָׂמַח rejoice; (Pi) gladden [śā/máḥ] 156

שָׂנֵא hate; (Qal and Pi part) adversary, enemy [śā/nḗʾ] 148

(I) שָׁבַר break [šā/ḇár] 149

שְׁמֹנֶה, שְׁמֹנָה; (s m, f; pl) eight; שְׁמֹנִים eighty [šəmō/néh, šəmō/nấ; šəmō/nîm] 147

שֵׁנִי (ord) second [šē/nî] 156

D. Words Occurring 143 through 134 Times (26)

אָז; מֵאָז (adv) then; formerly, since [ʾāz; mē/ʾáz] 141

זֶבַח slaughter, sacrifice; (Pi) sacrifice [zā/ḇáḥ] 136

חָכָם (adj) wise [ḥā/ḵám] 138

(I) *חָלַל (Ni) be defiled; (Pi) pollute, profane; (Hi) begin [ḥā/lál*] 134

(I) חָנָה encamp [ḥā/nấ] 143

יַחַד; יַחְדָּו (n) community; (adv) together, at the same time [yá/ḥaḏ; yaḥ/dáw] 142

יַיִן wine [yá/yin] 141

(I) יָמִין right hand/side; south [yā/mîn] 139

יֵשׁ there is/are [yēš] 139

כְּמוֹ (rel particle) just like [kəmô] 139

כִּסֵּא seat, throne [kis/sḗʾ] 136

(I) מִסְפָּר (n) number [mis/pár] 134

(II) מַעַל (adj) upwards; (prep) above [má/ʿal] 138

מִשְׁכָּן dwelling, tabernacle [miš/kān] 139

(I) נוּחַ (v) rest, settle down, make quiet; (Hi) lay, deposit [nûªḥ] 143

(I) נַחַל torrent valley, wadi [ná/ḥal] 138

(I) נְחֹשֶׁת copper, bronze [nəḥṓ/šet] 139

(I) סוּס; סוּסָה (m; f) horse; mare [sûs; sû/sấ] 139

עֲבוֹדָה service [ʿăḇô/ḏấ] 143

(II) עֶרֶב evening [ʿé/reb] 134

פָּנָה turn about, turn aside [pā/nấ] 134

(II) קָרָא happen; (inf cstr as prep) against [qā/rấʾ] 139

רָדַף pursue, persecute [rā/ḏáp̄] 143

שֶׁ־ (pref rel particle) who, which; that (with *dāḡēš* in following cons) 139

שְׁמוּאֵל Samuel [šəmû/ʾēl] 139
שֶׁמֶשׁ sun [šé/meš] 134

E. *Words Occurring 133 through 121 Times (28)*

אוֹר light [ʾôr] 125

אֱמֶת trustworthiness, stability, truth [ʾĕmet] 127

(I) אַף (conj) also, even, the more so [ʾap̄] 130

(I) בּוֹשׁ be ashamed [bôš] 126

בְּכֹר, בְּכוֹר firstborn [bəkōr, bəkôr] 122

גָּדַל be(come) strong, great; (Pi) bring up, let grow, nourish [gā/ḏál] 122

חוֹמָה (city) wall [ḥô/mâ] 133

חִזְקִיָּה; חִזְקִיָּהוּ Hezekiah [ḥiz/qiy/yấ; ḥiz/qiy/yắ/hû] 131

חֵמָה heat; rage, wrath; poison [ḥē/mấ] 126

חֲצִי half [ḥăṣî] 123

חֹק prescription, rule [ḥōq] 128

חָשַׁב (v) account, regard, value [ḥā/šáb] 124

יְהוֹנָתָן Jonathan [yəhô/nā/ṭắn] 124

כֶּבֶשׂ; כִּבְשָׂה (m; f) young ram; ewe-lamb [ké/beś; kib/śấ] 129

(I) כֹּחַ strength, power [kṓᵃḥ] 125

כֶּבֶשׂ; כִּשְׂבָּה Cf [ké/śeb; kiś/-bâ]

לָכַד seize, capture [lā/ḵáḏ] 121

נָגַשׁ draw near, approach [nā/ḡaš] 125

(I) נָשִׂיא prince [nā/śîʾ] 133

עַמּוֹן; עַמּוֹנִי Ammon; (gent) Ammonites [ʿam/môn; ʿam/mô/nî] 122

(I) עֶצֶם (s, coll) bone [ʿé/ṣem] 123

פֶּן־ (conj) lest [pen-] 133

קָבַץ assemble, gather together [qā/báṣ] 127

קָבַר bury [qā/ḇár] 132

קָהָל assembly, congregation [qā/hál] 123

שָׁאַר remain; (Ni, Hi) be left over [šā/ʾár] 133

שָׁכַן (v) tent, dwell, settle [šā/kán] 130

שָׁלַךְ (Hi) throw, cast [šā/láḵ] 125

F. *Words Occurring 120 through 112 Times (27)*

אֱדוֹם; אֱדוֹמִי Edom; (gent) Edomite(s) [ʾĕḏôm; ʾăḏô/mî] 112

אָחוֹת sister [ʾā/ḥôṯ] 114

(I) בָּטַח trust; fall to the ground? be reckless (II?) [bā/ṭáḥ] 119

בָּכָה weep [bā/ḵấ] 114

(II) *יָדָה (Pi) throw, cast; (Hi, Hith) thank, praise, confess [yā/ḏấ*] 115

יָטַב be good (cf טוב, 4.B; (I) טוב, 1.D) [yā/ṭáḇ] 120

יִצְחָק Isaac [yiṣ/ḥáq] 112

יָשָׁר (adj) straight, right, upright [yā/šấr] 119

כָּבֵד (stat) be heavy, honored [kā/ḇéḏ] 114

לָבַשׁ put on, clothe [lā/ḇáš] 113

לִקְרַאת (inf cstr as prep) over against, opposite [liq/rá't] 120

לָשׁוֹן tongue [lā/šốn] 117

מִגְרָשׁ pasture, untilled ground; produce [miḡ/rấš] 115

מַמְלָכָה kingdom [mam/lā/ḵấ] 117

נָבָא (Ni, Hith) prophesy [nā/ḇấ'] 115

נָהָר river, stream [nā/hấr] 117

פְּרִי fruit; offspring [pərî] 119

צֶדֶק righteousness; what is right, just [ṣé/ḏeq] 116

קָדוֹשׁ (adj) holy [qā/ḏốš] 115

קָטַר (Pi) send an offering up in smoke; (Hi) make smoke [qā/ṭár] 116

רֶכֶב chariot, chariotry [ré/ḵeb] 120

שָׂרַף burn [śā/ráp̄] 117

שָׁלֵם (stat) be whole, complete; (Pi) repay; (Hi) make peace with [šā/lḗm] 117

שֹׁמְרוֹן Samaria (2 times in Aramaic) [šōm/rốn] 112

שָׁפַךְ pour out [šā/p̄áḵ] 116

שֶׁקֶר lie, falsehood, deception [šé/qer] 113

תּוֹעֵבָה abomination [tô/'ē/ḇấ] 118

G. Words Occurring 111 through 100 Times (27)

אַבְשָׁלוֹם Absalom ['aḇ/šā/lốm] 107

(I) *אָמֵן (Ni) be steady, firm, trustworthy, faithful; (Hi) believe ['ā/mḗn*] 100

בִּלְתִּי (n) non-existence; (adv) not; (prep) except [bil/tî] 111

בָּמָה high place, funerary installation [bā/mấ] 103

(I) בַּעַד; בְּעַד (n) distance; (prep) behind, through, for (the benefit of) [bá/'aḏ] 101

(I) גָּאַל redeem [gā/'ál] 104

גִּלְעָד; גִּלְעָדִי Gilead; (gent) Gileadites [gil/'áḏ; gil/'ā/dî] 108

(I) הֵן (dem interj) behold!; (conj) if (cf הִנֵּה, 1.B) [hēn] 100

חֻקָּה statute, prescription [ḥuq/qấ] 104

יָרָבְעָם Jeroboam [yā/roḇ/-'ám] 104

יָתַר (Ni, Hi) be left, remain [yā/ṯár] 106

כָּנָף wing [kā/nấp̄] 110

כָּפַר cover; (Pi ext) expiate [kā/p̄ár] 102

מַרְאָה sight, appearance [mar/'éh] 103

נֶגֶב the dry country; south, Negev [né/ḡeb] 110

נָחַם (Ni) be sorry, repent; (Pi) comfort, console [nā/ḥám] 108

עַמּוּד pillar, column ['am/mûd̄] 111

עָפָר dry earth, dust ['ā/p̄ár] 110

פַּעַם foot, step; time [pá/'am] 111

רוּץ run [rûṣ] 103

רֹחַב breadth [rṓ/ḥab̄] 101

רָעָב hunger, famine [rā/'áb̄] 103

(II) רַק (adv) only [raq] 108

שַׁבָּת sabbath, rest [šab/bát̄] 106

שָׁכַח forget [šā/k̄áḥ] 102

שְׁלִישִׁי (ord) third; (fract) one-third [šəlî/šî] 107

תָּמִיד (n) continuance; (adv) continually, regularly [tā/mîd̄] 104

SECTION 4: HEBREW WORDS OCCURRING FROM 99 THROUGH 50 TIMES (313)

A. *Words Occurring 99 through 93 Times (26)*

אַחְאָב Ahab [ʾaḥ/ʾáb] 93

אֹרֶךְ length [ʾó/rek] 95

גֵּר stranger [gēr] 93

הָפַךְ turn, overturn [hā/pák] 95

זָנָה commit fornication; play the harlot [zā-nấ] 95

(I) חַיָּה (s or pl coll) animals [ḥay/yấ] 97

חָלָל (n, adj) slain, struck dead [ḥā/lắl] 94

(I) חֲמוֹר (male) ass [ḥămôr] 97

(I) חָרָה be(come) hot, burning, angry [ḥā/rấ] 94

טָהוֹר (adj) clean, pure [ṭā/hôr] 95

טָהֵר be clean, pure [ṭā/hḗr] 94

יַעַן (prep) on account of; (conj) because [yá/ʿan] 93

(I) יֶתֶר remainder [yé/ter] 96

(I) כֶּרֶם vineyard [ké/rem] 93

(I) *מָלַט (Ni) escape; (Pi) save, deliver [mā/láṭ*] 95

מְעַט (adj) (a) few; (n) a little [mǝ/ʿaṭ] 96

עוֹר skin, leather [ʿôr] 99

עֹז, עָז strength, power, might [ʿōz, ʿāz] 94

עֵשָׂו Esau [ʿē/śáw] 96

פֶּשַׁע rebellion, revolt, transgression [pé/šaʿ] 93

(I) רָעַע be wicked, evil [rā/ʿáʿ] 99

שָׂבַע satisfy, be satiated [śā/báʿ] 97

שִׂמְחָה joy, rejoicing [śim/ḥấ] 94

שְׁבִיעִי (ord) seventh [šǝbî/ʿî] 96

שָׁמֵם (stat) be astonished; be desolate [šā/mḗm] 95

שָׁרַת (Pi) minister to, serve [šā/ráṯ] 98

B. *Words Occurring 92 through 86 Times (31)*

אֱמֹרִי (gent) Amorite(s) [ʾĕmō/rî] 86

בָּעַר consume, burn (I?); graze (II?) [bā/ʿár] 87

דֶּלֶת door [dé/let] 87

דַּעַת knowledge [dá/ʿat] 91

הָמוֹן tumult, turmoil, multitude [hā/mốn] 86

זְרוֹעַ arm, forearm [zǝrôᵃ/ʿ] 91

(I) חֵלֶב fat [ḥé/leb] 92

(I) חָפֵץ please, delight, take pleasure [ḥā/p̄éṣ] 86

טוֹב be good, pleasant (cf יָטַב, 3.F; (I) טוּב, 1.D) [ṭôb̄] 90

טָמֵא; טְמֵאָה (adj, m; f) unclean [ṭā/mḗ'; ṭəmē/'ā́] 88

יְהוֹשָׁפָט Jehoshaphat [yəhô/šā/p̄āṭ] 86

יֶלֶד; יַלְדָּה (s m; f) male child, boy; girl [yé/leḏ; yal/dā́] 92

(I) כְּרוּב cherub [kərûb̄] 92

(I) כַּשְׂדִּים Chaldea; (gent) Chaldean (9 times in Aramaic) [kaś/dîm] 89

מַלְכוּת dominion; kingdom [mal/kûṯ] 91

נְבוּכַדְנֶאצַּר Nebuchadnezzar (spelled 5 ways in MT; 31x Aramaic) [nəbû/kaḏ/ne'ṣ/ṣár] 91

סָגַר shut, close; (Hi) deliver up, give in one's power [sā/ḡár] 90

(I) עֵבֶר side, region; opposite side ['é/b̄er] 91

(I) עָנָן clouds ['ā/nán] 86

(I) עֵצָה advice, counsel ['ē/ṣā́] 89

פֵּאָה side, rim, corner; piece? (II?); luxury? (III?) [pē/'ā́] 86

קֶדֶם; קֵדֶם in front, east; east(ward) [qé/ḏem; qē/ḏem] 87

קָצֶה end, border, extremity [qā/ṣéh] 90

רְאוּבֵן; רְאוּבֵנִי Reuben; (gent) Reubenite [rə'û/b̄én; rə'û/b̄ē/nî] 87

שִׁיר sing [šîr] 88

שִׁיר; שִׁירָה (m; f) song [šîr; šî/rā́] 91

שִׁית put, place [šîṯ] 87

שֶׁלֶם final (or peace) offering [šé/lem] 87

שָׁמַד (Ni) be destroyed, exterminated; (Hi) exterminate [šā/máḏ] 90

שֶׁקֶל *shekel* (unit of weight) [šé/qel] 88

תָּמִים (adj) whole, entire; blameless [tā/mím] 91

C. *Words Occurring 85 through 79 Times (27)*

אָוֶן wickedness, iniquity ['ắ/wen] 80

אוֹצָר supply, store-house, treasure ['ô/ṣár] 79

(I) אוֹת sign ['ôṯ] 79

אֲרִי; אַרְיֵה (m; m and f) lion ['ărî; 'ar/êh] 83

גָּד; גָּדִי Gad; (gent) Gadites [gāḏ; gā/ḏî] 85

(I) *גוּר sojourn [gûr*] 81

דָּנִיֵּאל Daniel (52 times in Aramaic section of Daniel) [dā/niy/yḗ'l] 81

הֵיכָל palace, temple [hê/kāl] 80

זָכָר man; male (animal) [zā/kár] 82

חֹשֶׁךְ darkness [ḥṓ/šek] 82

יָעַץ give counsel, advice [yā/'áṣ] 82

לָמַד learn; (Pi) teach [lā/mád] 85

(I) *מָהַר (Pi) hasten [mā/hár*] 83

מָכַר sell [mā/kár] 81

(II) מָשַׁל rule, govern [mā/šál] 82

סָתַר (Ni, intrans) conceal, hide; (Hi, trans) hide (someone) [sā/tár] 83

(III) עֵדָה ;עֵדוּת warning sign, reminder; precept, commandment [ʿē/dút; ʿē/dā́] 83

עָזַר help, assist [ʿā/zár] 82

(II) עָנָה bend down, be afflicted, humble; (Pi) oppress, humiliate [ʿā/nā́] 79

(II) *פָּלַל (Hith) pray [pā/lál*] 80

קָלַל be slight, trifling, swift; (Pi) declare cursed; (Hi) make light [qā/lál] 82

קָרְבָּן offering, gift [qor/bắn] 80

רָחוֹק (adj) far, distant; (n) distance [rā/hṓq] 85

רֹעֶה (Qal part) shepherd [rō/ʿéh] 84

שׁוֹר bull(ock), steer [šôr] 79

(I) שָׁחַט slaughter, kill [šā/hát] 85

שָׁקָה (Hi) give to drink [šā/qā́] 79

D. *Words Occurring 78 through 75 Times (28)*

בַּרְזֶל iron [bar/zél] 76

גּוֹרָל lot; (ext) allotment [gô/rắl] 78

דָּנִי ;דָּן Dan; (gent) Danites [dān; dā/nî] 78

חֶבְרוֹן Hebron [heb/rôn] 77

חָלָה be(come) weak, sick [hā/lâ] 77

(I) חָנַן be gracious to, favor; (Hith) implore favor or compassion [hā/nán] 77

יְשׁוּעָה deliverance, salvation [yəšû/ʿâ] 78

(I) מָאַס reject [mā/ʾás] 75

מָאתַיִם (du) two hundred [mā/ʾtá/yim] 77

מִקְנֶה possession (of land, cattle) [miq/néh] 76

מִשְׁמֶרֶת (n) guard, obligation, service [miš/mé/ret] 78

גֶּגַע blow, assault; plague [né/ḡaʿ] 78

נָצַב (Ni) take one's stand, be stationed (I?); wretched? (II?) [nā/sáb] 75

(III) *עוּר arouse, awake [ʿûr*] 76

עָנִי (adj) afflicted, poor [ʿā/nî] 76

עָרַךְ arrange, set in order [ʿā/rák] 75

(I) צוּר boulder, (large) rock [sûr] 75

(II) צַר adversary, foe [sar] 76

(I) קָנָה acquire, buy [qā/nâ]
78

קָרוֹב; קְרוֹבָה (adj m; f) near, imminent [qā/rôḇ; qərô/ḇâ] 78

קֶרֶן horn [qé/ren] 76

קֶשֶׁת bow (weapon); (met) rainbow [qé/šeṯ] 76

רָכַב ride [rā/ḵáḇ] 78

(I) שָׂכַל have success; (Hi) understand [śā/ḵál] 75

שָׁלָל plunder, booty [šā/lál] 76

תְּפִלָּה prayer [təp̄il/lâ] 78

תְּרוּמָה tribute, contribution, heave-offering [tərû/mâ] 77

תֵּשַׁע, תִּשְׁעָה; תִּשְׁעִים (s m, f; pl) nine; ninety [tḗ/šaʿ, tiš/ʿâ; tiš/ʿîm] 77

E. *Words Occurring 74 through 71 Times (28)*

אֵלִיָּה, אֵלִיָּהוּ Elijah [ʾē/liy/yâ, ʾē/liy/yá/hû] 71

אֶלְעָזָר Eleazar [ʾel/ʿā/zár] 72

אָסַר bind; (Ni, Pu) be fettered, imprisoned [ʾā/sár] 71

אֶרֶז (trad) cedar [ʾé/rez] 73

בֶּטֶן belly, womb [bé/ṭen] 72

(I) בְּרָכָה blessing [bərā/ḵâ] 71

גָּבַהּ (stat) be high [gā/ḇáh] 74

(I) הֶבֶל breath; vanity, idol(s) [hé/ḇel] 73

זָעַק cry out; (Ni) called to arms (cf צָעַק, 4.I) [zā/ʿáq] 73

זָר (adj) strange, different; illicit [zār] 71

חָזָה see, perceive [ḥā/zâ] 72

חֶרְפָּה reproach, disgrace [ḥer/pâ] 73

לְבָנוֹן Lebanon [ləḇā/nốn] 71

לִין* spend the night, lodge [lîn*] 71

מַדּוּעַ (interr adv) wherefore? why? [mad/dûaʿ] 72

מִזְרָח sunrise, east [miz/ráḥ] 74

מִקְדָּשׁ sanctuary [miq/dáš] 74

מֵת (adj) dead [mēṯ] 72

סֶלָה *selah* (unexplained technical term of music or recitation) [sé/lāh] 74

(II) עֵד; עֵדָה (m; f) witness [ʿēḏ; ʿē/ḏâ] 72

עוֹף (coll) flying creatures; fowl, insects [ʿôp̄] 71

עֵז goat; goathair [ʿēz] 74

(I) פָּלָא* (Ni) be extraordinary, wonderful [pā/láʾ*] 71

(I) צָרָה distress [ṣā/râ] 72

(I) קִיר wall [qîr] 74

רָחַץ wash (oneself) [rā/ḥáṣ] 72

שָׁבַת cease, rest [šā/ḇáṯ] 71

שׁוֹפָר ram's horn, trumpet [šô/p̄ár] 72

F. Words Occurring 70 through 66 Times (28)

אֲבִימֶלֶךְ Abimelech ['ăḇî-mé/leḵ] 67

אֲחֻזָּה landed property ['ăḥuz/zấ] 66

אַלּוּף (adj) familiar; (n) confidant (I); tribal chief (II) ['al/lûp̄] 69

בּוֹר cistern [bôr] 69

בֵּית(־)אֵל Bethel [bêṯ(-)-'ḗl] 70

בַּל (neg) not; surely? (II?) [bal] 66

גֶּבֶר (I) young man; strong man [gé/ḇer] 66

חֲלוֹם dream [ḥălôm] 66

חֵן charm, favor; grace [ḥēn] 68

כִּכָּר loaf of bread; talent; environs (all circular) [kik/kắr] 67

כְּסִיל (I) (adj) insolent (spiritual); stupid, dull (practical things) [kəsîl] 70

כְּפִי; לְפִי (conj) according to, as; so that [kəp̄î; ləp̄î] 67

כָּתֵף shoulder(-blade) [kā/ṯḗp̄] 67

כְּפִי Cf לְפִי

מִדְיָן; מִדְיָנִי Midian; (gent) Midianite (II) [miḏ/yán; miḏ/yā/nî] 67

מָלֵא (adj, n, pred adj) full [mā/lḗ'] 67

מָשַׁח anoint [mā/šáḥ] 70

נָבַט* (Pi, Hi) look at, regard [nā/ḇáṭ*] 70

עֵמֶק valley ['ḗ/meq] 68

פֹּה; פּוֹ; פֹּא here [pōh; pô; pō'] 68

פָּרַשׂ (trans) spread out; (met) flaunt [pā/ráś] 67

קֶבֶר grave [qé/ḇer] 67

קָדִים east side, east [qā/ḏîm] 69

קֵץ end; limit, boundary [qēṣ] 67

רָפָא heal (someone) [rā/p̄ắ'] 67

שְׁאֵרִית remainder [šə'ē/rît] 66

שֻׁלְחָן table [šul/ḥán] 70

תָּקַע drive, thrust; strike [tā/qá'] 67

G. Words Occurring 65 through 63 Times (24)

אַבְנֵר Abner ['aḇ/nḗr] 63

אָחַז (I) seize, hold fast ['ā/ḥáz] 63

אִשֶּׁה offering by fire ['iš/šéh] 65

בִּלְעָם (I) Balaam [bil/'ám] 64

גִּבְעָה (I) hill; (cultic) high place [giḇ/'ấ] 63

חֵלֶק (II) part, portion [ḥḗ/leq] 65

יְאֹר (great) river (Nile, Euphrates) [yə'ōr] 64

יוֹאָשׁ Joash [yô/'áš] 64

יָצַר form, shape, fashion [yā/ṣár] 64

כָּשַׁל stumble, totter [kā/šál] 63

מִיכָה, מִיכָא; מִיכָיְהוּ Micah [mî/ḵấ, mî/ḵắ'; mî/ḵā/yəhû] 63

(I) נַעֲרָה young girl, maid [na!/ʿărā] 63

נָצַח (Pi) lead; supervise [nā/ṣáḥ] 65

נָצַר watch, guard [nā/ṣár] 63

פּוּץ (intrans) scatter, disperse [pûṣ] 65

צִדְקִיָּהוּ ;צִדְקִיָּה Zedekiah [ṣid̄/qiy/yấ; ṣid̄/qiy/yấ/hû] 63

צָלַח (be) strong, effective; succeed [ṣā/láḥ] 65

רִיב contend, plead (a case) [rîb̠] 64

שְׁאוֹל *sheol*, underworld [šə'ôl] 65

שָׁכַם (den; Hi) rise early [šā/ḵám] 65

(II) שְׁכֶם Shechem [šəḵem] 64

שִׁפְחָה female slave [šip̄/ḥấ] 63

תָּמַם be complete [tā/mám] 64

תָּפַשׂ seize, take hold of [tā/p̄áś] 64

H. Words Occurring 62 through 58 Times (31)

אֶבְיוֹן (adj) poor, oppressed ['eb̠/yốn] 61

אַחֲרִית end, outcome ['a!/ḥărît] 61

אִיּוֹב Job ['iy/yôb̠] 58

אֵיךְ (interr) how? (cf אֵיכָה, 5.V) ['êḵ] 60

אֱלִישָׁע Elisha ['ĕlî/šấ'] 58

אָסָא Asa ['ā/sấ'] 58

אֵצֶל (n) side; (prep) beside ['é/ṣel] 61

אָרַר curse ['ā/rár] 59

(I) בָּרַח run away, flee [bā/ráḥ] 62

בָּשָׁן Bashan [bā/šán] 60

גְּבוּרָה strength [gəb̠û/rấ] 62

דּוֹד beloved, lover [dôd̠] 59

דָּרַךְ tread; (Hi) stamp firm [dā/ráḵ] 61

חַג ;חָג procession; feast, festival [ḥāḡ; ḥaḡ] 60

חָמָס violence, wrong [ḥā/mắs] 60

חִתִּי ;חֵת Heth; (gent) Hittite(s) [ḥēt̠; ḥit/tî] 62

יֵהוּא Jehu [yē/hûˀ] 58

(I) מָגֵן shield [mā/ḡḗn] 59

מָרְדֳּכַי Mordecai [mor/dŏḵái] 60

נֶדֶר ,נֵדֶר vow [né/d̠er, nĕ/d̠er] 60

נָחַל obtain, receive property [nā/ḥál] 59

(I) נֵסֶךְ ,נֶסֶךְ libation [né/seḵ, nĕ/seḵ] 60

(II) עֲרָבָה desert, plain [ʿărā/b̠ấ] 61

צָרַר wrap up (I); be hostile toward (II) (cf (I) צוּר, 5.J) [ṣā/rár] 61

קְטֹרֶת smoke (of sacrifice); incense [qət̠ő/ret] 61

קָנֶה (measuring) reed, tube [qā/néh] 62

קָרַע tear up, away [qā/ráˀ] 62

רִיבָה ;רִיב (m; f pl) contention, suit; legal speech [rîb̠; rî/b̠ấ] 62

רֵיחַ odor, scent [rêªḥ] 59

שֹׁפֵט (n, Qal part act) judge [šō/p̄ḗṭ] 58

תְּהִלָּה glory, praise [təhil/lā̂] 58

I. Words Occurring 57 through 55 Times (34)

אֶ֫דֶן* (pl) pedestal, socket ['é/den*] 55

אַלְמָנָה widow ['al/mā/nā̂] 55

אָמָה female slave ['ā/mā̂] 56

אֶסְתֵּר Esther ['es/tḗr] 55

אֹרַח way, path ['ó/raḥ] 57

גֶּ֫פֶן vine [gé/p̄en] 55

זָרַע sow [zā/rá'] 56

חָזָק (adj) hard, strong [ḥā/záq] 56

(I) חִיל* be in labor [ḥîl*] 57

(II) חָלַק divide, apportion; (Pi) scatter (III?) [ḥā/láq] 56

טֶ֫רֶם; בְּטֶ֫רֶם (neg) not yet; (conj, prep) before [ṭé/rem; bəṭé/rem] 56

יָבֵשׁ (stat) be dry; (intrans) dry up [yā/b̄ḗš] 55

יְהוֹיָדָע Jehoiada [yəhô/yā/-d̄á'] 56

יָכַח* (Ni) dispute; (Hi) reprove [yā/ḵáḥ*] 56

(I) יַ֫עַר thicket [yá/'ar] 57

יְרִחוֹ Jericho [yəri/ḥô] 57

יִשְׁמָעֵאל; יִשְׁמְעֵאלִי Ishmael; (gent) Ishmaelite [yiš/mā/'ḗ'l; yiš/mə'ē'/lî] 56

מִזְמוֹר psalm [miz/môr] 57

מַחֲשָׁבָה thought [ma!/ḥăšā/b̄â] 56

מְנַצֵּחַ conductor? (Pi part of נָצַח) [mənaṣ/ṣḗªḥ] 57

נָטַע (v) plant [nā/ṭá'] 57

סֶ֫לַע rock [sé/la'] 57

סֹפֵר scribe, writer [sō/p̄ḗr] 55

(I) עָמָל distress, trouble; effort ['ā/mál] 55

פָּדָה buy (off), ransom [pā/d̄â] 56

פָּעַל make, do [pā/'ál] 57

פָּרָשׁ horsemen; horse [pā/ráš] 57

רְבִיעִי (ord) fourth; (fract) one-fourth [rəb̄î/'î] 55

רָחַק be(come) far (away), distant [rā/ḥáq] 57

(II) רָמָה Ramah [rā/mâ] 57

רָצוֹן pleasure; favor [rā/ṣôn] 56

שָׂעִיר (n) he-goat (II); (adj) hairy (I) [śā/'îr] 55

שָׁדַד devastate, lay waste [šā/d̄ád̄] 56

שְׁמָמָה horror, desolation [šəmā/mâ] 56

J. Words Occurring 54 and 53 Times (29)

אָבָה accede, accept ['ā/b̄â] 54

אֱמוּנָה steadiness ['ĕmû/nâ] 53

גָּמָל camel [gā/mál] 54

דָּבַק stick, cling to [dā/b̄áq] 54

דְּבַשׁ honey [dəb̄aš] 54

הָמָן Haman [hā/mán] 54

(I) חָדַל cease, desist [ḥā/ḏál] 53

חָדָשׁ (adj) new, fresh [ḥā/ḏắš] 53

חֵץ arrow [ḥēṣ] 54

חָתַת be shattered; (ext) filled with terror [ḥā/ṯát] 53

יָצַק dish up (food); pour out (liquid) [yā/ṣáq] 53

(III) *יָרָה (Hi) instruct, teach [yā/rā̃*] 54

יְרִיעָה curtain, tent (fabric) [yərî/ʿấ] 54

כּוּשׁ; כּוּשִׁי Cush; (gent) Cushite [kûš; kû/šî̃] 54

כָּעַס (be) irritated, angry [kā/ʿás] 54

(II) לָבָן Laban [lā/ḇán] 54

(I) מִדָּה (n) measure [mid/dấ] 53

(I) מַצָּה unleavened bread [maṣ/ṣấ] 53

מָרוֹם height [mā/rốm] 54

סֹלֶת fine wheat flour [sŏ/leṯ] 53

עֶלְיוֹן upper; Most High [ʿel/yốn] 53

עֶרְוָה nakedness [ʿer/wấ] 53

צָדוֹק Zadok [ṣā/ḏốq] 53

צֵל shadow, shade [ṣēl] 53

צָעַק cry out (cf זָעַק, 4.E) [ṣā/ʿáq] 54

קָטֹן (adj) small, insignificant [qā/ṭŏ́n] 54

שְׂמֹאל left (side); left hand [śəmō̃ʾl] 54

(II) שָׂרָה; שָׂרַי Sarah; Sarai [śā/rā̃; śā/rái] 53

שֵׁן tooth; (ext) crag [šēn] 53

K. *Words Occurring 52 through 50 Times (27)*

אַחֲרוֹן (adj) behind; (adv) last [ʾa!/ḥărốn] 50

אַיֵּה (interr) where? [ʾay/yḗh] 52

אֵילָם; אוּלָם vestibule [ʾê/lám; ʾû/lám] 50

בָּקַע (v) split [bā/qáʿ] 51

בְּתוּלָה virgin [bəṯû/lấ] 51

(I) חָרַם devote to the ban [ḥā/rám] 51

יֹאשִׁיָּה, יֹאשִׁיָּהוּ Josiah [yō̃/šiy/yấ, yō̃/šiy/yắ/hû] 51

יוֹמָם in the daytime [yô/mắm] 51

כָּבַס full (cloth); (Pi) wash [kā/ḇás] 51

מָדַד (v) measure [mā/ḏáḏ] 52

מוּסָר chastening, correction [mû/sắr] 50

מָחָר tomorrow [mā/ḥár] 52

(I) *נָדַח (Ni) be scattered [nā/ḏáḥ*] 51

נָכַר (Ni) pretend; (Hi) investigate, recognize [nā/kár] 50

נַפְתָּלִי Naphtali [nap̄/tā/lî̃] 50

נָשַׂג (Hi) overtake [nā/śáḡ] 50

עֲמָלֵק; עֲמָלֵקִי Amalek; (gent) Amalekite [ʿămā/lḗq; ʿămā/lē/qî̃] 51

פָּרַץ make a breach; burst out [pā/ráṣ] 50

פָּרַר* (Hi) break out, burst forth; shake (II?) [pā/rár*] 50

קֶרֶשׁ plank [qé/reš] 51

רֵאשִׁית beginning, first [rē'/šît] 51

רְחַבְעָם Rehoboam [rəḥab/'ám] 50

רָנַן shout (for joy) [rā/nán] 52

(I) רָצָה be pleased with; like [rā/ṣâ] 50

שָׁוְא (adj, n) worthless-(ness); (adv) in vain [šāw'] 52

תָּעָה wander off, stagger [tā/'â] 50

תִּפְאֶרֶת (f) ornament, decoration [tip̄/'é/ret] 51

SECTION 5: HEBREW WORDS OCCURRING FROM 49 THROUGH 10 TIMES (1248)

A. *Words Occurring 49 and 48 Times (30)*

(I) אֹמֶר saying, word [ʾḗ/mer] 49

(I) אֵפֹד *ephod* (priestly garment; cult object) [ʾē/p̄ṓḏ] 49

בָּגַד treat faithlessly [bā/ḡáḏ] 49

בַּעֲבוּר on account of, for the sake of, because of, in order that [ba!/ʿăḇûr] 49

(I) בָּרָא create [bā/rắ] 48

גָּאוֹן loftiness; pride [gā/ʾṓn] 49

גִּלּוּל* (pl) idols [gil/lûl*] 48

(I) דֶּבֶר (bubonic) plague [dé/ḇer] 49

(II) דַּל (adj) mean, scanty; (n) poor [dal] 48

הוֹי (interj) alas! woe! [hôy] 48

(I) הֵנָּה (adv; spacial) hither, here; (temporal) until now [hḗn/nâ] 49

הַרְבֵּה (adv) great number, many, much [har/bḗh] 49

(II) חֶבֶל rope; (ext) measure, plot [ḥé/ḇel] 49

טַבַּעַת ring, signet-ring [ṭab/bá/ʿat] 49

יָצַב* (Hith) take one's stand, position, stand (firm); appear, arrive [yā/ṣáḇ*] 48

(I) מִגְדָּל tower [miḡ/dắl] 49

מַכָּה blow, wound [mak/kâ] 48

מִשְׁקָל weight [miš/qắl] 49

נְבֵלָה corpse [nəḇē/lâ] 48

נָגַף injure, strike [nā/ḡáp̄] 49

סָמַךְ support [sā/mák̲] 48

(I) עֲבוּר* (alw with pref בַּ-) Cf בַּעֲבוּר [ʿăḇûr*] 49

(I) עַד eternity, always [ʿaḏ] 48

(I) פַּחַד trembling, terror [pá/ḥaḏ] 49

פֶּסַח Passover (festival, sacrifice) [pé/saḥ] 49

(I) קָצִיר crop, harvest [qā/ṣî̄r] 49

שַׂק goathair cloth, sackcloth; sack [śaq] 48

שְׁבִי (those who are/that which is) taken captive [šəḇî] 48

שַׁדַּי (adj) Almighty [šad/dái] 48

תְּכֵלֶת purple wool [tək̲ḗ/let] 49

B. *Words Occurring 47 and 46 Times (26)*

אָשָׁם guilt, wrong; guilt offering [ʾā/šăm] 46

גֹּאֵל redeemer [gō/ʾēl] 46

גַּיְא valley [gayʾ] 47

גָּרַשׁ banish, divorce, drive out (I?); toss up (II?) [gā/ráš] 47

חֲנִית spear [ḥănît] 47

(II) חָרֵשׁ (stat) be deaf; (Hi) be silent [ḥā/rḗš] 47

לִשְׁכָּה hall [liš/kâ] 47

מָאֵן* (Pi) refuse, refuse to [mā/ʾán*] 46

מַעֲלָה ascent [ma!/ʿălâ] 47

מִשְׁכָּב couch, bed [miš/káb] 46

מִשְׁתֶּה (drinking-) feast [miš/téh] 46

מָתְנַיִם (du) loins [mot/ná/-yim] 47

נָכְרִי (adj) foreign, strange; (n) foreigner [nok/rî] 46

נְעוּרִים youth [nə/û/rîm] 47

סָלַח forgive [sā/láḥ] 46

(I) עֵזֶר; עֶזְרָה (s m; f) support, help, (ext or coll) helper(s) [ʿḗ/zer; ʿez/râ] 47

עָצַר restrain, detain [ʿā/ṣár] 46

פָּגַע encounter, meet; entreat [pā/ḡáʿ] 46

(II) צָפָה arrange; (Pi) overlay [ṣā/p̄â] 46

(I) קָוָה wait, await [qā/wâ] 47

קוֹמָה height, stature [qô/mâ] 46

(I) קָטָן (adj) small, young (-er, -est) [qā/ṭắn] 47

קָשַׁב be sharp, attentive [qā/šáb] 46

רָחַם* (Pi) show love for [rā/ḥám*] 47

רָצַח kill [rā/ṣáḥ] 47

שָׁבָה take captive [šā/bâ] 47

C. *Words Occurring 45 and 44 Times (27)*

(II) אוּלַי (adv) perhaps [ʾû/lái] 45

אֹכֶל food [ʾṓ/kel] 45

אֶשֶׁר* (pl) fortune; happiness [ʾé/šer*] 45

(I) בָּחוּר young man [bā/ḥûr] 45

גִּיל* shriek ecstatically, shout with joy [gîl*] 45

חָגַר gird, put on a belt [ḥā/ḡár] 44

חָלָב milk [ḥā/láb] 44

חָלַץ take off; (Qal part pass) ready for battle [ḥā/láṣ] 44

יָרֵא (adj) fearing, afraid of [yā/rḗʾ] 45

יִרְאָה (n) fear, reverence [yir/ʾâ] 45

מְדִינָה province, district [mədî/nâ] 45

מוֹשָׁב dwelling place [mô/šáb] 44

מָרָה be rebellious, obstinate [mā/râ] 45

מֶרְכָּבָה chariot [mer/kā/b̄ấ] 44

(I) מַשָּׂא carrying, burden [maś/śấ] 45

נָגִיד chief, leader [nā/ḡîd] 44

נוֹרָא awe-inspiring [nô/rấ] 44

(I) נֵר lamp [nēr] 45

סָרִיס eunuch, court official [sā/rîs] 45

עוּד* (Pi) surround [ˁûd̠*] 45

עָמַד* (alw with suffix; prep) with (cf עִם, 1.B) [ˁim/māḏ*] 45

קָשַׁר tie up, bind [qā/šár] 44

רוּעַ* (Hi) shout [rûªˁ*] 44

רָפָה become slack; sink down [rā/p̄ấ] 45

רֶשַׁע; רִשְׁעָה (s m; f) wrong, injustice, guilt [ré/šaˁ; riš/ˁấ] 45

שֶׂה lamb, kid [śeh] 44

(I) שֶׁבֶר, שֵׁבֶר breaking, fracture; interpretation [šé/b̠er, šḗ/b̠er] 44

D. Words Occurring 43 and 42 Times (40)

אוֹר* shine [ˀôr*] 43

(I) אֱנוֹשׁ men [ˀĕnôš] 42

אֶפֶס (n) end, nothingness; (particle of neg; adv) without [ˀé/p̄es] 42

(II) בַּד* (pl) poles; shoots [bad̠*] 42

בָּדַל* (Ni) separate oneself [bā/d̠ál*] 42

בָּזָה despise [bā/zấ] 43

בָּזַז (v) plunder [bā/záz] 42

(I) בֶּטַח safety; (adv) securely [bé/ṭah] 43

בָּלַל moisten; confuse, confound [bā/lál] 43

גּוֹלָה exiles; deportation, exile [gô/lấ] 42

הָרָה conceive, become pregnant [hā/rấ] 43

הָרַס demolish [hā/rás] 43

זוּב* (v) flow; suffer a discharge [zûb̠*] 42

(I) זָמַר* (Pi) sing [zā/már*] 43

(I) זָרָה scatter [zā/rấ] 42

חָרְבָּה desert, waste [ḥor/bấ] 42

טַף children [ṭap̄] 42

יָחַל* (Pi, Hi) wait [yā/ḥál*] 42

(I) יָסַד found, lay the foundations of [yā/sád] 43

(I) יָסַר* (Qal part) teach; (Ni) teach oneself, take advice [yā/sár*] 42

יָתוֹם orphan [yā/t̠ốm] 42

כִּנּוֹר lyre [kin/nốr] 42

לוּחַ tablet; board, plank [lûªḥ] 43

מַחֲלֹקֶת portion, share [ma!/ḥălố/qet] 42

מְנוֹרָה lampstand [mənô/rấ] 42

מַעֲלָל* (pl) deed, act [ma!/ˁălál*] 42

(I) מְעָרָה cave [məˁā/rấ] 42

מָתַי (interr) when? [mā/-t̠ái] 43

נָוֶה pasturage, abode (I?); praiseworthy?, comely? (II?) [nā/wéh] 42

נִיחֹחַ (adj) soothing, tranquillizing [nî/ḥôᵃḥ] 43

נֶצַח (I) luster, glory [né/ṣaḥ] 43

נָקִי (adj) free from, exempt [nā/qî] 43

נָתַץ tear down, demolish [nā/táṣ] 42

פָּשַׁט take off [pā/šáṭ] 43

צַוָּאר neck [ṣaw/wắr] 42

קִנְאָה passion [qin/’ắ] 43

רְחֹב, רְחוֹב (I) broad open place, plaza [rəḥōḇ, rəḥôḇ] 43

שָׁנִי (I) crimson, scarlet [šā/nî] 42

תְּבוּאָה (n) produce, yield [təḇû/’ắ] 43

תְּבוּנָה intelligence, skill [təḇû/nắ] 42

E. Words Occurring 41 and 40 Times (30)

אַהֲבָה (I) love [’a!/hăḇắ] 40

אָזַן* (I) (Hi) listen (to) [’ā/zán*] 41

אָחוֹר back; (adv) behind [’ā/ḥôr] 41

אָמַץ (I) be strong [’ā/máṣ] 41

אָרַב lie in ambush [’ā/ráḇ] 41

אֲשֵׁרָה Asherah; cult-post [’ăšē/rá] 40

בָּלַע (I) (v) swallow [bā/láʿ] 40

בְּרִיחַ bar [bərîᵃḥ] 41

גָּבֹהַּ high [gā/ḇóᵃh] 40

גַּן garden [gan] 41

דָּגָן grain [dā/ḡán] 40

דַּי sufficiency; enough [dai] 40

חָמַל feel compassion for [ḥā/mál] 41

חָרוֹן anger [ḥā/rôn] 41

חָרַף (II) (v) taunt, reproach [ḥā/ráp] 40

יָפֶה (adj) handsome, beautiful [yā/p̄éh] 41

כָּבֵד (I) (n; adj) heavy, weighty; rich [kā/ḇéd] 40

מוּט* waver, reel, totter [mûṭ*] 41

נוּעַ* (v) shake, totter [nûᵃʿ*] 41

נָחָה (v) lead [nā/ḥá] 40

נָטַשׁ leave, abandon [nā/ṭáš] 40

נָקָה* (Ni) be free [nā/qắ*] 41

עֹל yoke [ʿōl] 40

פָּשַׁע (v) revolt, rebel [pā/šáʿ] 41

צָדַק be in the right, have a just case [ṣā/dáq] 41

צִפּוֹר (I) (coll) birds [ṣip/pôr] 40

רָגַז (intrans) shake, quake [rā/ḡáz] 41

שֹׂנֵא enemy [śō/né’] 41

שָׁקַט have peace, be at peace [šā/qáṭ] 41

תּוֹלֵעָה worm [tô/lē/’ắ] 41

F. Words Occurring 39 and 38 Times (29)

אָבַל mourn [ˈā/bál] 39

אֵיפָה ephah (grain measure) [ˈê/p̄â] 38

אָן; אָנָה (interr) where? from where? [ˈān; ˈắ/nâ] 38

אַרְגָּמָן purple [ˈar/gā/mán] 39

בָּהַל* (Ni) be terrified [bā/hál*] 39

גָּנַב steal [gā/náb] 39

זַיִת olive (fruit and tree) [zá/yit] 38

חֶדֶר (dark) room, bedroom [ḥé/der] 38

חֵיק lap, bosom [ḥêq] 38

חֵפֶץ delight, joy [ḥḗ/p̄eṣ] 39

חָרַד tremble, shudder [ḥā/rád] 39

חָרָשׁ craftsman [ḥā/ráš] 38

כָּלַם* (Ni) be shamed, disgraced [kā/lám*] 38

מָטָר rain [mā/ṭár] 38

מְלֹא fulness, what fills [məlôˈ] 38

מִלָּה word, message [mil/lâ] 38

(I) מַר (adj) bitter; (adv) bitterly [mar] 39

(I) מִרְמָה deceit, fraud [mir/mâ] 39

מָשִׁיחַ anointed (one) [mā/šî-aḥ] 39

(I) מָשָׁל saying, proverb [mā/šál] 39

פֹּעַל deed, work [pō/ˈál] 38

(I) צֵלָע rib [ṣē/láˈ] 39

קָהַל* (Ni, intrans) assemble [qā/hál*] 39

רַחֲמִים compassion [ra!/ḥămîm] 39

(I) שַׁמָּה astonishment, horror [šam/mâ] 39

(III) שֵׁשׁ (Egyptian) linen [šēš] 38

תְּאֵנָה fig (-tree) [təˈē/nâ] 39

תּוֹלְדוֹת descendants, generations [tô/lē/dôt] 39

תִּירוֹשׁ wine [tî/rôš] 38

G. Words Occurring 37 and 36 Times (38)

(I) אִי coast, region [ˈî] 36

אָלָה (n) curse [ˈā/lâ] 37

אִמְרָה word, utterance [ˈim/râ] 37

אָשַׁם be(come) guilty [ˈā/šám] 36

(I) בְּאֵר well, pit [bəˈḗr] 37

בִּינָה insight [bî/nâ] 37

גָּמַל finish; (Ni) be weaned [gā/mál] 37

חָסָה seek refuge [ḥā/sâ] 37

(I) חָרֵב (stat) be dry [ḥā/rḗb] 36

טֻמְאָה (state of cultic) uncleanness [ṭum/ˈâ] 37

יָקָר (adj) rare, costly; noble [yā/qắr] 36

יֵשַׁע salvation, liberation [yḗ/šaˈ] 36

כּוֹכָב star [kô/kā̲b] 37

כּוּל* seize; (Hi) contain; (Pilp) clasp [kûl*] 37

כָּנַע* (Ni) be subdued, humbled [kā/náʿ*] 36

כָּרַע bend the knee, kneel [kā/ráʿ] 36

לָקַט gather (up), glean [lā/qáṭ] 37

(I) מִבְצָר fortress, fortified city [mib/ṣár] 37

מוּל (n) front; (as prep) front of, towards [mûl] 36

מוֹפֵת sign, omen [mô/p̄ét] 36

מָעוֹז fortress [mā/ʿôz] 36

מַצֵּבָה pillar [maṣ/ṣē/b̠â] 36

מָשַׁךְ seize, pull [mā/šák̠] 36

(I) נוּף* (Hi) move back and forth [nûp̄*] 37

נֵכָר foreign land [nē/k̠ár] 36

נָסָה* (Pi) (put someone to the) test [nā/sâ*] 36

(I) עֵדֶר flock, herd [ʿé/d̠er] 37

עֳנִי misery, affliction [ʿŏnî] 36

עָשַׁק oppress, do wrong [ʿā/šáq] 37

עֹשֶׁר riches [ʿó/šer] 37

פִּלֶגֶשׁ; פִּילֶגֶשׁ concubine [pi!/lé/ḡeš; pî/lé/ḡeš] 37

(I) צָפָה keep guard, watch [ṣā/p̄â] 37

קָשֶׁה (adj) hard, severe [qā/šéh] 36

שָׂחַק play (act) clumsy; laugh [śā/ḥáq] 36

שׁוֹעֵר gatekeeper [šô/ʿér] 37

תֵּבֵל continent(s) [tē/b̠él] 36

תְּהוֹם (n) deep, ocean depths [təhốm] 36

תְּרוּעָה shout (of alarm, joy) [tərû/ʿâ] 36

H. Words Occurring 35 and 34 Times (41)

אוֹפַן wheel [ʾô/p̄án] 35

אָרַךְ be long [ʾā/rák̠] 34

אָתוֹן she-ass [ʾā/t̠ôn] 34

גֹּרֶן threshing floor [gó/ren] 34

(I) גֶּשֶׁם rain [gé/šem] 35

דָּג; דָּגָה (m; f coll) fish [dāḡ; dā/ḡâ] 34

(I) הַב יְהַב Cf יְהַב, 5.H [hab]

הָמָה make noise, roar [hā/mâ] 34

זֹנָה (female) prostitute [zō/nâ] 35

(I) זָרַק scatter [zā/ráq] 34

חָבָא* (Ni) hide (oneself), be hidden [ḥā/b̠áʾ*] 34

חָזוֹן vision [ḥā/zôn] 35

חֵטְא fault, sin [ḥēṭʾ] 35

חָסִיד (one who is) faithful, devout [ḥā/sîd̠] 35

יְהַב (impv) give; (interj) come on! [yə/háb̠] 34

יָנַק suck(le), nurse [yā/náq] 34

יָרֵךְ upper thigh [yā/rék̠] 34

כָּכָה (adv) so, thus [ká/k̠â] 35

כַּלָּה daughter-in-law; bride [kal/lâ] 34

לְאֹם people [lə/ʾōm] 35

(I) מָחָה wipe off; wipe out [mā/ḥâ] 34

מַלְכָּה queen [mal/kấ] 35

מָעַל be unfaithful [mā/ʿál] 35

מִשְׁנֶה second, double [miš/néh] 35

נָקַם take vengeance [nā/qám] 35

סֵתֶר hiding place; garment [sḗ/ter] 35

עֶבְרָה arrogance [ʿeḇ/rấ] 34

עֵגֶל (bull-) calf [ʿḗ/ḡel] 35

(I) עַם kinsman, relative [ʿam] 34

עָרֵל (adj) uncircumcised [ʿā/rḗl] 35

צָפַן (v) hide; treasure up [ṣā/p̄án] 34

צָרַעַת skin disease (not leprosy) [ṣā/rá/ʿat] 35

צָרַף smelt, refine [ṣā/ráp̄] 34

קָנָא (Pi) be envious of; arouse jealousy [qā/nấʾ] 34

קָצָה end, border [qā/ṣấ] 35

קָצַף be(come) angry [qā/ṣáp̄] 34

(I) קָצַר reap, harvest [qā/ṣár] 35

רָשַׁע be(come) guilty [rā/šáʿ] 35

שְׂעֹרָה barley [śə/ʿō/rấ] 34

(II) תִּקְוָה expectation, hope [tiq/wấ] 34

תְּשׁוּעָה salvation [təšû/ʿấ] 34

I. Words Occurring 33 and 32 Times (38)

אַרְמוֹן palace [ʾar/mṓn] 33

(II) גְּדוּד raiding party [gəḏûḏ] 33

חָבַשׁ bind, bind on; saddle [ḥā/ḇáš] 33

חִנָּם (adv) without compensation; in vain [ḥin/nắm] 32

חָתַן become related by marriage; (Qal part) father- (mother-) in-law [ḥā/tán] 33

טַבָּח butcher, cook [ṭab/bắḥ] 32

טוֹב (n) goodness, the best [ṭûḇ] 32

(I) יוֹנָה dove [yô/nấ] 33

יְמָנִי right (hand); southern [yəmā/nî] 33

(I) יָרָה throw; shoot [yā/rấ] 33

כָּחַד (Ni) be hidden [kā/ḥáḏ] 32

כֶּלֶב dog [ké/leḇ] 32

לְבוּשׁ garment; (coll) clothes [ləḇûš] 32

מְאוּמָה anything (at all) [məʾû/mấ] 32

(I) *מוּל circumcise [mûl*] 32

מִזְרָק sprinkling basin [miz/ráq] 32

מָחֳרָת (n) the following day; (adv) on the next day [mo!/ḥŏrắt] 32

מֵעֶה (du cstr) bowels, abdomen [mē/ʿéh] 32

מַעֲשֵׂר tithe [ma!/ʿăśḗr] 32

(I) נָשַׁק kiss [nā/šáq] 32

עַוְלָה wickedness [ʿaw/lấ] 32

(I) *עָמָה (alw pref with ‑לְ; adv) just like; (prep) close to, at [ʿum/mấ*] 32

עֵרֶךְ layer, row; accessories [ʿế/reḵ] 33

עֹרֶף neck, nape [ʿố/rep̄] 33

עֵשֶׂב (coll) green plants, herbs [ʿế/śeḇ] 33

פְּנִימִי (adj) inner [pənî/mî] 33

פְּקֻדָּה appointment, service [pəqud/dấ] 33

(I) פָּרַח sprout; break out [pā/ráḥ] 32

(I) צַד side [ṣad] 33

צָמַח (v) sprout [ṣā/máḥ] 33

קְלָלָה curse [qəlā/lấ] 33

(II) רֶחֶם, רַחַם womb [ré/ḥem, rá/ḥam] 32

(I) רִמּוֹן pomegranate [rim/mốn] 32

(I) רִנָּה shout of joy [rin/nấ] 33

שְׁבוּת; שְׁבִית (carrying off to) captivity, imprisonment [šəḇûṯ; šəḇîṯ] 32

שֹׁרֶשׁ root [šố/reš] 33

תּוֹדָה (song, sacrifice of) thanksgiving [tô/dấ] 32

תַּחְתִּי; תַּחְתּוֹן (adj) lower, lowest; (n) the lowest [taḥ/tî; taḥ/tốn] 32

J. Words Occurring 31 Times (26)

אֵי (interr) where? [ʾê]

אֳנִיָּה ship [ʾŏniy/yấ]

אֶצְבַּע finger [ʾeṣ/báʿ]

בְּכִי weeping [bəḵî]

גָּג roof [gāḡ]

(I) דָּמָה be (a)like [dā/mấ]

חַלּוֹן window (-opening) [ḥal/lốn]

טַל dew, light rain [ṭal]

טָמַן hide; set up secretly [ṭā/mán]

יָלַל (Hi) howl, wail [yā/lál]

(I) כּוֹס (drinking-) cup [kôs]

כָּזָב lie, falsehood [kā/záḇ]

כִּלְיָה (pl) kidney [kil/yấ]

כְּפִיר young lion [kəp̄îr]

מִין kind, species [mîn]

נָאַף commit adultery [nā/ʾáp̄]

נָדַר make a vow [nā/ḏár]

(I) נָחָשׁ serpent [nā/ḥáš]

סֻכָּה thicket; hut [suk/kấ]

(II) עָב cloud(s) [ʿāḇ]

עָצוּם (adj) mighty, vast [ʿā/ṣûm]

פֶּסֶל idol [pé/sel]

(I) *צוּר tie up, gather [ṣûr*]

שִׂמְלָה mantle, wrapper (cf שַׂלְמָה, 5.V) [śim/lấ]

שְׁבוּעָה oath [šəḇû/ʿấ]

שָׁטַף wash away, wash off [šā/ṭáp̄]

K. Words Occurring 30 and 29 Times (41)

בָּחַן test [bā/ḥán] 30

בַּמָּה, בַּמֶּה (interr pr) how? [bam/mấ, bam/méh] 29

בָּרָד hail [bā/rắd] 29

בְּשֶׂם; בֹּשֶׂם balsam shrub [bó-/śem; bé/śem] 30

בֹּשֶׁת shame [bó/šet] 30

גָּזַל tear off, pull off, seize [gā/zál] 30

הָדָר ornament [hā/dắr] 30

(I) זִמָּה plan; infamy [zim/mấ] 29

חִטָּה wheat [ḥiṭ/ṭấ] 30

חָמַם be(come) warm, hot [ḥā/mám] 29

חֲצֹצְרָה trumpet [ḥăṣō/ṣǝrấ] 29

(I) חֵרֶם ban, (what is) banned [ḥḗ/rem] 29

חָשַׂךְ restrain, withhold [ḥā/śák] 29

יָעַד designate [yā/ʿád] 29

כְּלִמָּה (n) disgrace, insult [kǝlim/mấ] 30

כֻּתֹּנֶת tunic [kut/tó/net] 29

(I) לָבָן (adj) white [lā/bắn] 29

מַאֲכָל food; fodder [ma!/ʾăkắl] 30

מִטָּה bed, couch [miṭ/ṭấ] 29

מָנָה (v) count [mā/nấ] 29

מָנַע retain, withhold [mā/náʿ] 29

(I) מַעַל unfaithfulness [má/ʿal] 29

נִדָּה; נִידָה menstrual flow; excretion [nid/dấ; nî/-dấ] 30

(I) נָהַג drive, lead [nā/hág] 30

סִיר (cooking-) pot [sîr] 30

סָפַד mourn, sound a lament [sā/p̄ád] 30

עָלַם (Qal part) secret (faults); (Ni) be hidden [ʿā/lám] 29

עִשָּׂרוֹן tenth part [ʿiś/śā/rôn] 30

עַתּוּד* (pl) ram, he-goat; (met) leader [ʿat/tûd̄*] 29

פִּנָּה corner [pin/nấ] 30

פָּרָה bear fruit [pā/rấ] 29

(I) קֶצֶף anger, rage [qé/ṣep̄] 29

קִרְיָה city, town [qir/yấ] 30

רָבַץ lie down, crouch [rā/báṣ] 30

(I) רָעַשׁ quake, shake [rā/ʿáš] 30

שֵׂעָר (coll) hair [śē/ʿár] 29

(I) שָׂרִיד survivor [śā/rîd] 29

שְׁמִינִי (ord) eighth [šǝmî/nî] 30

שָׁפֵל (stat) be low, sink [šā/p̄él] 29

שִׁקּוּץ abominable idol; abomination [šiq/qûṣ] 29

תְּנוּפָה waving, shaking; (ext) wave-offering [tǝnû/p̄ấ] 30

L. *Words Occurring 28 and 27 Times (54)*

אַדִּיר (adj) mighty; (n, pl) nobles [ʾad/dîr] 27

אָוָה* (Ni?) be beautiful, lovely; (Pi) want, crave [ʾā/wấ*] 27

(I) אֱוִיל (adj) foolish; (n) fool, simpleton [ʾĕwîl] 27

בַּז (n) plunder (act and objects of) [baz] 27

בְּלִיַּעַל wickedness [bəliy/yá/ʿal] 27

בָּשַׁל ripen, cook; (Pi) cook, boil [bā/šál] 28

זָקֵן (stat) be old [zā/qḗn] 27

(II) חָבַר become allies, unite [ḥā/bár] 28

חָכַם be(come) wise [ḥā/ḵám] 27

חָלַם be(come) strong; (Qal, Hi) dream [ḥā/lám] 28

(I) חָלַף pass by, follow each other [ḥā/láp̄] 27

חֲמִישִׁי (ord) fifth; (fract) one-fifth [ḥămî/šî] 27

חָקַר spy out, investigate [ḥā/qár] 27

חָתַם seal up, confirm [ḥā/tám] 27

יוֹבֵל ram; year of jubilee [yô/ḇḗl] 27

יָצַת kindle, burn up [yā/ṣát] 27

יָרֵחַ moon [yā/rḗaḥ] 27

יְרֵכָה rear, back side [yərē/ḵắ] 28

יָשַׁר be (go) straight [yā/šár] 27

כַּפֹּרֶת (performance of) re-conciliation; (trad) cover, lid [kap̄/pṓ/reṭ] 27

לִיץ boast; (Hi) mock, be a spokesman (inter-preter) [lîṣ] 28

מָבוֹא; מוֹבָא entrance [mā/ḇôˇ; mô/ḇắˀ] 27

(I) מוֹצָא outlet; what comes out [mô/ṣắˀ] 27

מוֹקֵשׁ trap [mô/qḗš] 27

מוֹשִׁיעַ helper, deliverer [mô/šîˀaˁ] 27

(II) מֶלַח salt [mé/laḥ] 28

מְסִלָּה road, highway [məsil/lắ] 27

מְעִיל robe [məˁîl] 28

(II) נֵבֶל, נֶבֶל harp? [nḗ/ḇel, né/ḇel] 27

נְדָבָה free will; voluntary gift [nəḏā/ḇắ] 27

נָדַד flee, wander [nā/ḏáḏ] 27

נָדִיב willing; (one who is) noble [nā/ḏîḇ] 27

נוּד wander [nûḏ] 27

נְקָמָה vengeance, revenge [nəqā/mắ] 27

נָתַק tear away, draw (one) away [nā/táq] 27

(I) *עוּף fly; (Poˁl) soar; (Hithpoˁl) fly off [ˁûp̄*] 27

עֲשִׂירִי (ord) tenth; (fract) one-tenth [ˁăśî/rî] 28

פֶּחָה governor [pe!/ḥắ] 28

פָּלַט escape [pā/láṭ] 27

פְּלֵיטָה (n) escape [pəlê/ṭắ] 28

(I) פָּתָה be inexperienced, naive [pā/ṭắ] 28

קָרָה happen, come about [qā/rắ] 27

קָשָׁה be hard, heavy [qā/šắ] 28

רְכוּשׁ property, goods [rəḵûš] 28

שׂוּשׂ rejoice [śûś] 27

שָׂטָן accuser, adversary; the Satan [śā/ṭán] 27

(I) שָׂכָר wages, reward [śā/ḵár] 28

שִׁטָּה acacia (tree, wood) [šiṭ/ṭắ] 28

(I) שָׁלֵם (adj) uninjured, safe; complete [šā/lḗm] 28

שְׁמוּעָה news, report [šəmû/ʿâ] 27

שִׁשִּׁי (ord) sixth; (fract) one-sixth [šiš/šî] 27

תֵּבָה ark, chest [tē/ḇâ] 28

תָּלָה hang [tā/lâ] 27

תֹּם integrity, complete-ness [tōm] 28

M. *Words Occurring 26 and 25 Times (53)*

אִוֶּלֶת foolishness [ʾiw/wé/let] 25

אֵיפֹה (interr) where? [ʾê/p̄ṓh] 25

אָמֵן (interj) amen! surely! [ʾā/mḗn] 25

אָפָה bake [ʾā/p̄â] 25

אֵפוֹא (adv) then, so [ʾē/p̄ṓ] 25

בָּצוּר (Qal part pass) im-pregnable [bā/ṣûr] 25

בֶּרֶךְ knee [bé/reḵ] 25

גָּבַר excel; (Hi) be strong [gā/ḇár] 25

דְּמוּת likeness [dəmûṯ] 25

(I) הָגָה mutter, growl [hā/ḡâ] 25

הוֹן wealth [hôn] 26

חִיצוֹן (adj) outer [ḥî/ṣṓn] 25

חָצֵב quarry, hew (out), stir? (II?) [ḥā/ṣéḇ] 25

(I) חָרַשׁ plow; engrave [ḥā/ráš] 25

חֹשֶׁן breast-plate (of the high priest) [ḥṓ/šen] 25

טוּר row, course (of building stone) [ṭûr] 26

טָרַף tear in pieces [ṭā/ráp̄] 25

יָגַע grow weary [yā/ḡáʿ] 26

(I) יָשַׁן go to sleep; sleep [yā/šán] 25

כַּעַס, כַּעַשׂ irritation, anger [ká/ʿas, ká/ʿaś] 25

מַגֵּפָה plague, torment [mag/gē/p̄â] 26

מְכוֹנָה place, abode; stand [məḵô/nâ] 25

מָסָךְ covering, curtain [mā/sáḵ] 25

(I) מַסֵּכָה cast image; drink of-fering [mas/sē/ḵâ] 26

מָצוֹר affliction (I?); fortification (II?) [mā/ṣôr] 25

מָרַד (v) rebel [mā/ráḏ] 25

נֵזֶר consecration (of the Nazirite) [né/zer] 25

נֹכַח (prep) in front of, opposite; (n) what lies opposite [nó/kaḥ] 25

נֶשֶׁר eagle, vulture [né/šer] 26

נָתִיב; נְתִיבָה (s m; f) path [nā/tîḇ; nəti/ḇâ] 26

(I) *סוּג deviate, be disloyal [sûḡ*] 25

(III) סַף threshold [sap̄] 25

עֲגָלָה wagon, cart [ʿăḡā/lâ] 25

עִוֵּר (adj) blind [ʿiw/wḗr] 26

עֲלִילָה deed, action [ʿălî/lấ] 25

(I) עָשָׁן smoke [ʿā/šấn] 25

(I) פַּח bird trap [paḥ] 25

פָּחַד tremble [pā/ḥáḏ] 25

פָּרַד (Qal part pass) outspread; (Ni) divide, (intrans) separate [pā/ráḏ] 26

פָּרֹכֶת curtain [pā/rố/keṯ] 25

פִּתְאֹם (adv) suddenly [piṯ/ʾốm] 25

צוֹם (act, time of) fasting [ṣôm] 25

קָדַם (Pi) be in front, walk at the head [qā/ḏám] 26

רָגַל slander; (Pi) spy out; (Tifel) teach (someone) to walk [rā/ḡál] 26

(I) רָדָה tread (winepress); rule [rā/ḏấ] 25

רָחַב open wide, broaden [rā/ḥáḇ] 25

שְׁאָר remainder, remnant [šə/ʾār] 26

(II) שֹׁד violence, destruction [šōḏ] 25

שֹׁטֵר officer, record-keeper [šō/ṭếr] 25

שָׁלַף draw (sword); take off [šā/láp̄] 25

שִׁלְשׁוֹם (idiom) three (days ago, day before yesterday) [šil/šốm] 25

תּוּר go about, explore; (ext) spy out [tûr] 25

(I) תְּחִנָּה supplication (for mercy); pardon, mercy [təḥin/nấ] 25

N. Words Occurring 24 Times (30)

אֵבֶל (rites of) mourning [ʾḗ/ḇel]

אוֹי (interj) woe!; (n) woe [ʾôy]

אֵיד disaster, calamity [ʾêḏ]

אַרְבֶּה locust [ʾar/béh]

בָּשַׂר (Pi) bring news [bā/śár]

גָּוַע expire, die, perish [gā/wáʿ]

דִּין (v) judge; bring justice [dîn]

(I) הוֹד height, majesty [hôḏ]

זִכָּרוֹן reminder [zik/kā/rốn]

חוּס pity, be troubled about [ḥûs]

חֳלִי illness, suffering [ḥŏlî]

(II) חֶלְקָה piece of land, plot of ground [ḥel/qấ]

יָתֵד peg, tent-peg [yā/ṯéḏ]

כָּבָה be extinguished [kā/ḇấ]

כֹּתֶרֶת (column-) capital [kō/ṯé/reṯ]

מְלוּכָה kingship [məlû/kấ]

נָאַץ reject, disdain [nā/ʾáṣ]

נָזָה be sprinkled; (intrans) spatter [nā/zấ]

(I) נָסַךְ pour out [nā/sáḵ]

נְשָׁמָה blowing; breath [nəšā/mấ]

סַעַר; סְעָרָה (s m; f) gale, windstorm [sá/ʿar; sə/ā/rấ]

פָּלִיט, פָּלֵיט fugitive(s) [pā/lîṭ, pā/lêṭ]

פְּקוּדִים directions, orders [piq/qû/dîm]

(I) רָבַב be(come) great, much, numerous [rā/ḇáḇ]

רוּשׁ* be poor [rûš*]

שַׁחַר dawn [šá/ḥar]

O. Words Occurring 23 Times (35)

אָבִיר, אַבִּיר strong, powerful [ʼā/ḇîr, ʼab/bîr]

(III) בַּד linen [bad]

בֶּצַע a piece cut off [bé/ṣaʻ]

גָּלַח* (Pi) shave [gā/láḥ*]

דִּמְעָה (s coll) tears [dim/ʻâ]

זֵכֶר mention, remembrance [zé/ḵer]

(I) חוֹל sand, mud [ḥôl]

חָסֵר (stat) lack, be lacking; diminish [ḥā/sḗr]

(I) חָפַר dig [ḥā/p̄ár]

חָפַשׂ search out, check [ḥā/p̄áś]

יָעַל* (Hi) help, be of use [yā/ʻál*]

(I) יִצְהָר olive oil [yiṣ/hár]

כָּהַן* (Pi) perform the duties of priest [kā/hán*]

כִּיּוֹר (wash-) basin, pot [kiy/yôr]

(I) מָדוֹן; מִדְיָן quarrel, dispute [mā/dôn; miḏ/yán]

מִישׁוֹר level ground, plain [mî/šôr]

שָׁכֹל (stat) be bereaved (of children) [šā/ḵól]

שָׁנָה (v) change; repeat [šā/nâ]

תּוֹכַחַת reprimand [tô/ḵá/ḥat]

(I) תֵּימָן south; southern area [tê/mán]

מַס compulsory labor, *corvée* [mas]

מַעְיָן spring [maʻ/yán]

מִקְרָא convocation [miq/rắ]

מְרִי obstinacy [mərî]

נָגַשׂ beat, drive [nā/ḡáś]

נָקַב pierce; designate [nā/qáḇ]

(I) סָכַךְ isolate, cover [sā/ḵáḵ]

עַז (adj) defiant, shameless [ʻaz]

(I) עֲטָרָה wreath, crown [ʻă/ṭā/rá]

עָשִׁיר (adj) wealthy, rich [ʻā/šîr]

פְּסִיל* (pl) idols [pā/sîl*]

צָהֳרַיִם (du) midday, noon [ṣo!/hŏrá/yim]

שֹׁחַד gift; bribe [šó/ḥad]

שַׁחַת pit(-fall), grave [šá/ḥat]

שֵׁכָר intoxicating drink, beer? [šē/ḵár]

שֵׁנָה sleep [šē/nâ]

תּוֹצָאוֹת (pl) exits; starting point [tô/ṣā/ʼôṯ]

תְּחִלָּה beginning [təḥil/lâ]

תְּמוֹל yesterday [təmôl]

P. Words Occurring 22 Times (37)

(III) אַיִל gatepost? [ʼá/yil]

אַיִל; אַיָּלָה fallow deer (buck; doe) [ʼay/yál; ʼay/yā/lâ]

אֵפֶר ashes, dust ['é/p̄er]

גָּדַע cut off [gā/dáʿ]

(I) דָּמַם stand (keep) still [dā/mám]

דָּת regulation, law [dāṯ]

הִין *hin* (liquid measure) [hîn]

(II) *זָהַר (Ni) be warned; (Hi) warn [zā/hár*]

זַעַם (n) curse [zá/ʿam]

טֶרֶף prey; food [ṭé/rep̄]

יוֹעֵץ counsellor [yô/ʿéṣ]

כָּחַשׁ become lean; (Pi) deny, deceive [kā/ḥáš]

כָּלָה destruction, anni- hilation [kā/lâ]

לוּ, לוּא (imprec) if only; O that…might [lû, lûʾ]

מוֹלֶדֶת descendants, kindred [mô/lé/ḏet]

מַחְתָּה fire-pan [maḥ/tâ]

מָעַט be(come) few [mā/ʿáṭ]

נַעַל sandal [ná/ʿal]

נָפַץ smash; scatter (II?); (Ni) break up [nā/p̄áṣ]

נְקֵבָה (n, adj) female [nəqē/ḇâ]

סָקַל (v) stone [sā/qál]

עֲבֹת rope ['ăḇōṯ]

פֶּגֶר corpse [pé/ḡer]

פָּשָׂה (v) spread [pā/śâ]

(I) צָעִיר small (-er, -est); young (-er, -est) [ṣā/ʿîr]

קִיץ spend the summer [qîṣ]

רֶגַע tranquillity; moment [ré/ḡaʿ]

רֶשֶׁת (bird) net [ré/šeṯ]

שָׂשׂוֹן joy [śā/śôn]

שָׁוַע (Pi) cry for help [šā/wáʿ]

שָׁזַר (Ho part) twisted [šā/zár]

(I) שְׁכֶם shoulder(s) [šəkem]

שָׁעַן (Ni) lean (against); (met) depend (on) [šā/ʿán]

שָׁקַל weigh (out) [šā/qál]

שָׁקַף (Ni, Hi) look down [šā/qáp̄]

תַּזְנוּת obscene manner [taz/nûṯ]

תָּעַב (Ni) be loathed, abhorrent [tā/ʿáḇ]

Q. *Words Occurring 21 Times (40)*

אָתָה come ['ā/ṯâ]

בְּעוֹד while yet, as long as (cf עוֹד, 2.A) [bə/ʿôḏ]

(I) בָּרָק lightning [bā/ráq]

(I) גָּרַע shave; diminish [gā/ráʿ]

(II) זָנַח reject [zā/náḥ]

(I) *חוּשׁ hurry [ḥûš*]

חָמַד desire, crave [ḥā/máḏ]

חֹתֵן father-in-law [ḥō/ṯén]

לְבֹנָה, לְבוֹנָה frankincense [lā/ḇō/- nâ, ləḇô/nâ]

(I) לְחִי chin, jawbone [ləḥî]

מְגִלָּה scroll [məḡil/lâ]

מוּם, מְאוּם blemish [mûm, mə'ûm]

מְנוּחָה rest, resting place [mənû/ḥấ]

מָסַס lose courage; (Ni) dissolve [mā/sás]

(II) מַשָּׂא utterance [maś/śấ’]

(I) מִשְׁחָה anointing [miš/ḥấ]

מַשְׁקֶה cup-bearer; well-irrigated land [maš/qéh]

(?) * מֹת (pl) men [mōṯ*]

נֵס signal pole; banner [nēs]

נָתַךְ gush forth, be poured out [nā/ták]

נָתַשׁ uproot, tear out [nā/táš]

סוֹד confidential conversation [sôḏ]

סָחַר pass through, wander around [sā/ḥár]

סָפָה take away [sā/p̄ấ]

(II) * סֶרֶן (pl) prince [sé/ren*]

עָוֶל wrong, injustice [ʿấ/wel]

עָנָו (K; adj) humble [ʿấ/nấw]

פָּקַח (v) open [pā/qáḥ]

פַּרְסָה (divided) hoof [par/sấ]

צוּם (v) fast [ṣûm]

צְעָקָה (n) cry, call for help [ṣəʿấ/qấ]

(I) רָחָב (adj) wide, broad [rā/ḥáḇ]

שָׂמֵחַ (adj) joyful, glad [śā/méᵃḥ]

שָׁאַג (v) roar [šā/ʾáḡ]

(II) שָׁבַר buy (food) [šā/bár]

שָׁגָה stray, go astray [šā/ḡấ]

שַׁד (du) breast [šaḏ]

שַׁחַק (coll) dust; clouds of dust? [šá/ḥaq]

תַּאֲוָה longing, desire [ta!/ʾăwấ]

תָּמַךְ grasp [tā/mák]

R. *Words Occurring 20 Times (33)*

אֱלִיל worthless; (ext) pagan gods [ʾĕlîl]

בִּקְעָה plain, broad valley [biq/ʿấ]

בְּרוֹשׁ (Phoenician) juniper [bərôš]

(I) גַּל heap [gal]

(I) חָבַל take (something) in pledge [ḥā/bál]

(II) חָלִיל (neg interj) be it far from [ḥā/lî̂l]

חָתָן son-in-law; bridegroom [ḥā/ṭán]

יָחַשׂ (Hith) be enrolled (in genealogical registry) [yā/ḥáś]

יָנָה be violent, oppress; (Hi) oppress [yā/nấ]

יְסוֹד foundation(-wall), base [yəsôḏ]

מְהֵרָה (n) speed, haste; (adv) quickly [məhē/rấ]

(II) *מוּשׁ withdraw; (Hi) remove [mûš*]

מְזוּזָה doorpost [məzû/zấ]

מַחְסֶה refuge [maḥ/séh]

מִקְלָט refuge, asylum [miq/láṭ]

מִשְׁמָר guard [miš/már]

עֲלִיָּה upper room, roof-chamber [ʿăliy/yā]

עָמָל labor, exert oneself [ʿā/mál]

עָרִיץ (adj) violent, mighty; (n) master [ʿā/rîṣ]

(I) עָתַר pray; (Ni) be moved by entreaties [ʿā/t̠ár]

(II) צִנָּה shield [ṣin/nā]

(I) צַר (adj) narrow; (n) distress [ṣar]

צָרַע (Qal, Pu part) suffering from a skin disease [ṣā/ráʿ]

קַיִץ summer; summer fruit [qá/yiṣ]

קָסַם practice divination [qā/sám]

שָׂגַב be (too) high; be fortified [śā/g̠áb̠]

שֵׂיב; שֵׂיבָה old age [śêb̠; śê/b̠ā]

שִׂיחַ be(come) concerned, consider [śîʾḥ]

שָׁבוּעַ week [šā/b̠ûªʿ]

שָׁכֵן inhabitant, neighbor [šā/k̠én]

שְׁפֵלָה the lowland(s) [šəp̄ē/lā]

תַּבְנִית shape, form; pattern [tab̠/nît̠]

תֹּהוּ wasteland, formlessness; nothingness [tó/hû]

S. *Words Occurring 19 Times (41)*

(I) אוּלָם (advs) on the other hand, however [ʾû/-lám]

(I) אָפִיק stream-channel [ʾă/p̄îq]

אַשְׁמָה guilt [ʾaš/mā]

בָּרַר purge out, sort; sharpen? (II?) [bā/rár]

גַּאֲוָה loftiness; haughtiness [ga!/ʾăwā]

גְּמוּל doings; recompense [gəmûl]

דִּין lawsuit [dîn]

זָקָן beard [zā/qán]

חַטָּא sinner; sinful [ḥaṭ/ṭáʾ]

חָקַק hew out; engrave [ḥā/qáq]

(II) *יָאַל (Hi) make a beginning [yā/ʾál*]

יֳפִי beauty [yŏp̄î]

לָאָה be(come) weary [lā/ʾā]

לֶהָבָה flame [le!/hā/b̠ā]

לַחַץ crowd, press; oppress [lā/ḥáṣ]

מָאוֹר luminary [mā/ʾôr]

מְזִמָּה plan, plot [məzim/-mā]

מֵישָׁרִים straightness, fairness [mê/šā/rîm]

מַעֲלֶה ascent, steep path [ma!/ʿăléh]

מַעֲרָכָה row; battle line [ma!/ʿărā/k̠ā]

(I) נָבֵל wither [nā/b̠él]

(I) נֹגַהּ brightness, shining [nó/g̠ah]

עָלֶה leaves, leaf [ʿā/léh]

עֵנָב grape (cluster) [ʿē/náb̠]

עַשְׁתֵּי (f) eleven(th) [ʿaš/têʾ]

(I) פֶּרֶץ breach, gap [pé/reṣ]

(I) פֶּתִי (adj) young, naïve [pé/t̠î]

רִיק* (v) empty out, draw (sword); muster [rîq*]

רָמַס trample, tread [rā/más]

רֹע bad quality [rṓaʿ]

רָעֵב (adj) hungry [rā/ʿéḇ]

רַעֲנָן (adj) luxuriant [ra!/ʿănán]

רָצַץ smash up; abuse [rā/ṣáṣ]

שָׂכַר hire [śā/ḵár]

שָׁאַב draw (water) [šā/ʾáḇ]

שְׁגָגָה error, inadvertence [šəḡā/ḡấ]

שׁוֹק thigh; (ext) leg [šôq]

שָׁכַר be(come) drunk(en) [šā/ḵár]

(I) שֶׁלֶג snow [šé/leḡ]

שָׁפָל (adj) deep, low; humble [šā/p̄ál]

תְּמֹרָה ornament of palm tree [ti!/mō/rấ]

T. *Words Occurring 18 Times (43)*

(I) אוֹן power, strength, wealth [ʾôn]

אָחַר delay, keep back [ʾā/ḥár]

אָכְלָה food [ʾok/lấ]

אָכֵן (interj) truly! indeed! [ʾā/ḵén]

אֹרֶב ambush [ʾō/réḇ]

בִּירָה citadel [bî/rấ]

גַּחֶלֶת live coals [ga!/ḥé/let]

דָּכָא* (Ni part) oppressed; (Pi) crush [dā/ḵấ*]

זְעָקָה cry, call for help [zəʿā/qấ]

זָרַח go forth, shine [zā/ráḥ]

חֵךְ palate [ḥēḵ]

חָסֵר (one who) lacks [ḥā/sér]

(I) חָצִיר grass [ḥā/ṣîr]

חָשַׁךְ be (grow) dark [ḥā/šáḵ]

יָבַל* (Hi) bring [yā/ḇál*]

כַּד jar [kaḏ]

(I) כָּלָא restrain [kā/lắ]

(II) כַּפְתּוֹר knob [kap̄/tṓr]

(I) לוּן* (Ni) murmur, grumble [lûn*]

לָעַג (v) ridicule [lā/ʿáḡ]

מַטָּה (adv) below, beneath [mát/ṭā]

מָעוֹן lair; dwelling [mā/ʿṓn]

(II) מְצוּדָה mountain stronghold [məṣû/ḏấ]

מָקוֹר spring, source [mā/qṓr]

מַקֵּל shoot, twig [maq/qél]

מֶרְחָק distance [mer/ḥáq]

(I) נָבָל (adj) foolish [nā/ḇál]

נָזַל trickle, flow; (Qal part act) brook, watercourse [nā/zál]

נָטַף drip [nā/ṭáp̄]

סוּת* (Hi) lead astray, seduce [sût*]

סָרַר be stubborn (I?) [sā/rár]

עָטָה (v) wrap, cover [ʿā/ṭấ]

(I) עָלַל* (Po) treat, deal with [ʿā/lál*]

(I) עָצַם be mighty; numerous [ʿā/ṣám]

(I) צְבִי ornament; glory [ṣəbî]

צַלְמָוֶת darkness [ṣal/má/wet]

(I) קִינָה dirge, lament [qî/nâ]

רָכַל* (Qal part) trader, merchant [rā/kál*]

שָׂכִיר (adj) rented, hired; (n) hired laborer, mercenary [śā/kîr]

שָׁחַח stoop, crouch [šā/ḥáḥ]

(I) שָׁקַד be awake, watch [šā/qád]

תַּחֲנוּן* supplication [ta!/ḥănûn*]

תָּכַן examine [tā/kán]

U. Words Occurring 17 Times (64)

אֶזְרָח native, citizen [ʾez/ráḥ]

אֵימָה terror, dread [ʾê/mâ]

אָסִיר; אַסִּיר prisoner [ʾā/sîr; ʾas/sîr]

בָּאַשׁ stink [bā/ʾáš]

בִּכּוּרִים first fruits [bik/kû/rîm]

בְּרֵכָה pond, pool [bərē/kâ]

גֹּבַהּ height [gó/bāh]

גְּבִיר; גְּבִירָה (s m) lord, master; (f) lady, mistress [gəbîr; gəbî/râ]

גַּנָּב thief [gan/náb]

(II) דָּמָה come to rest, end; (Ni ext?) be silent, destroyed (III?) [dā/mâ]

דָּרוֹם south; south wind [dā/rôm]

חֹזֶה vision [ḥō/zéh]

חִידָה riddle [ḥî/dâ]

(II) חֹמֶר mortar, cement; clay [ḥó/mer]

(II) חָפֵר (stat) be ashamed [ḥā/pér]

חָפְשִׁי (adj) freed, free [ḥop/šî]

חֶרֶשׂ clay, pottery [ḥé/reś]

יוֹצֵר potter, founder [yô/ṣér]

יְקָר preciousness; honoring, esteeming [yəqár]

כֵּן stand, base; place (IV?); (ext) position (V?) [kēn]

כְּתָב (n) document; register [kətāb]

כָּתַת beat fine, pound up [kā/tát]

מוּג* reel, melt [mûg*]

מָטַר* (Ni) be rained on; (Hi) have (make) rain fall [mā/tár*]

מָכוֹן place; support [mā/kôn]

מֶמְשָׁלָה dominion [mem/šā/lâ]

מִסְגֶּרֶת dungeon [mis/gé/ret]

מִשְׂגָּב high spot, refuge [miś/gáb]

מָשׂוֹשׂ joy [mā/śôś]

(I) מָשַׁל make up (say) a (mocking-) verse [mā/šál]

מִשְׁעָן, מַשְׁעֵן; מַשְׁעֵנָה, מִשְׁעֶנֶת (m; f) support [miš/ʿán, maš/ʿén; maš/ʿē/nâ, miš/ʿé/net]

(I) מַתָּנָה gift, present [mat/tā/nấ]

נָדַב urge on, prompt; (Hithp) volunteer [nā/ḏáḇ]

נֶזֶם ring [né/zem]

נָקָם (human) revenge; (divine) recompense [nā/qám]

(II) נָקַף make a (yearly) round [nā/qáp̄]

נָתִין* (pl) temple slave; bondsman [nā/tín*]

סֶגֶן* ,סְגָן* (pl) governor, prefect [sé/ḡen*, sā/ḡǎn*]

עָוָה do wrong [ʿā/wấ]

עָיֵף (adj) weary, faint [ʿā/yép̄]

עָלַז exult [ʿā/láz]

עָמֹק (adj) deep; (ext) impenetrable [ʿā/móq]

עָצָב* (pl) images, idols [ʿā/ṣáḇ*]

(I) עָרַב stand (as) surety (for) [ʿā/ráḇ]

עָשַׁר be(come) rich; (Hi) make someone rich [ʿā/šár]

פֶּרַח bud, flower [pé/raḥ]

צָמָא (n) thirst [ṣā/mấ]

קָדַר grow dark, turbid [qā/ḏár]

קָלוֹן shame [qā/lôn]

קְעָרָה dish [qəʿā/rấ]

רָמַשׂ swarm, teem [rā/máś]

רֶמֶשׂ (coll) small animals, reptiles [ré/meś]

רַעַשׁ quaking, commotion [rá/ʿaš]

רָקִיעַ plate; (met) firmament [rā/qîaʿ]

שְׂבָכָה net; lattice, grille [śəḇā/ḵấ]

שִׂנְאָה hate, hatred [śin/ʾấ]

(II) שָׁאוֹן din, uproar [šā/ʾôn]

שְׁאֵר flesh, food; blood-relation [šəʾêr]

(I) שׁוּשַׁן lily, lotus [šû/šán]

(III) שָׁלִישׁ third man in chariot; (ext) adjutant [šā/lîš]

שֵׁמַע hearsay, report [šḗ/maʿ]

תֶּבֶן straw, chaff [té/ḇen]

תֹּף timbrel, tambourine [tōp̄]

תְּשִׁיעִי (ord) ninth [təšî/ʿî]

V. Words Occurring 16 Times (64)

(II) אוֹב spirit (of the dead) [ʾôḇ]

אָזַר put on, gird [ʾā/zár]

אֵיכָה (interr) how? in what way? (cf אֵיךְ, 4.H) [ʾê/ḵấ]

(I) אֵלָה mighty tree [ʾē/lấ]

(I) אָמַל* (Pul) dry up [ʾā/mál*]

אָמְנָה; אָמְנָם, אֻמְנָם (adv) truly, surely; (with interr) really? [ʾom/nấ; ʾom/nǎm, ʾum/nǎm]

בֹּהֶן* thumb; big toe [bǒ/hen*]

בָּלָה become old and worn out [bā/lấ]

בִּלְעֲדֵי* (prep) apart from, except for [bal/ʿăḏê*]

בָּעַל (I) rule, own; marry [bā/ʿál]

בָּעַת* (Ni) be terrified [bā/ʿát*]

בָּצַע cut off [bā/ṣáʿ]

גְּדִי kid (goat) [gədî]

גַּל* (II) (pl) wave [gal*]

גַּנָּה garden [gan/nâ]

דְּבִיר (I) holy of holies [dəbîr]

דּוּשׁ* trample; thresh [dûš*]

הָרֶה (adj) pregnant [hā/réh]

זוּלָה (prep) except, besides; (conj) except that [zû/lâ]

חָגַג celebrate [hā/ḡáḡ]

חֶמְדָּה something desirable, excellent [ḥem/dâ]

חֹרֶב dryness, drought; desolation [ḥṓ/reb]

חָשָׁה be quiet [ḥā/šâ]

טָבַל dip [ṭā/bál]

יְגִיעַ labor, work; gain [yəḡîaʿ]

יָצַג* (Hi) set (down), place [yā/ṣáḡ*]

יֶקֶב wine-vat; winepress [yé/qeb]

כָּזַב lie; (Ni) prove to be a liar [kā/záb]

לָבוּשׁ (adj) clothed, dressed [lā/bûš]

לֵץ babbler, scoffer [lēṣ]

מַחֲצִית half [ma!/ḥăṣît]

מַטָּרָה target; (men on) guard [maṭ/ṭā/râ]

מַכְאֹב pain [mak/ʾṓb]

מִכְסֶה cover(ing) [mik/séh]

מִסְפֵּד mourning (rites) [mis/-pḗd]

מָרַר be bitter [mā/rár]

מַשָּׂאָה; מַשְׂאֵת lifting up [maś/śâ/ʾă; maś/ʾḗt]

נָזִיר (adj) dedicated; (n) Nazirite [nā/zîr]

נָשָׁא (I) lend, make a loan [nā/šâ]

נָשָׁא* (II) (Ni) be deceived [nā/šâ*]

נָשָׁה (II) Cf (I) נָשָׁא

סוּפָה (I) (storm-) wind [sû/p̄â]

סֹחֵר trader, merchant [sō/ḥḗr]

סַם* (pl coll) perfume [sam*]

עָנָה (IV) sing [ʿā/nâ]

עָרוֹם (adj) naked [ʿā/rṓm]

עָרְלָה foreskin [ʿor/lâ]

פָּרַע let (hang) loose [pā/ráʿ]

פֵּשֶׁת flax, linen [pḗ/šet]

צוּד* hunt [ṣûd*]

צִיָּה dry country, desert [ṣiy/yâ]

צֶמֶר wool [ṣé/mer]

קֶלַע* (II) (pl) curtain [qé/laʿ*]

קַשׁ stubble [qaš]

רְבָבָה very great multitude; ten thousand [rəbā/bâ]

רַב(-)שָׁקֵה (Assyrian office?) cupbearer [rab(-/)šā/qḗh]

רָגַם (v) stone (someone) [rā/ḡám]

רֵיקָם (adv) emptily [rê/qåm]

רַךְ (adj) tender, frail [rak]

שְׂחוֹק laughter [śəḥôq]

שֵׂכֶל, שֶׂכֶל insight, understanding [śé/kel, śé/kel]

(I) שַׂלְמָה mantle, wrapper (cf שִׂמְלָה, 5.J) [śal/mấ]

(I) שָׁוָה be(come) like, equal [šā/wấ]

שֶׁפֶט (pl) judgment; (ext) punishment [šé/p̄eṭ*]

W. Words Occurring 15 Times (48)

אַמְתַּחַת sack; load? [ʼam/tá/ḥat]

אָרֵךְ ; אֶרֶךְ (abs; cstr) slow, long [ʼā/rék̠; ʼé/rek̠]

גָּזַז shear (sheep), cut (hair) [gā/záz]

גֻּלָּה basin [gul/lấ]

גָּלוּת exile, deportation; exiles [gā/lût̠]

(I) גָּלַל roll [gā/lál]

גְּעָרָה (n) rebuke; threat [gəʽā/rấ]

גָּרָה (Pi) go to law [gā/rấ]

דֶּשֶׁן fat; fatty ashes [dé/šen]

(III) הָלַל be deluded [hā/lál]

חָצָה divide [hā/ṣấ]

יֹשֶׁר straightness, up-rightness [yṓ/šer]

כָּבַשׁ subdue, subject [kā/b̠áš]

כָּלִיל (adj) entire, whole; (n) entirety [kā/lîl]

מֹאזְנַיִם (du) scales, balance [mṓ/zəná/yim]

מִבְטָח trust, confidence [mib̠/ṭáḥ]

מוּר (Ni, intrans) change; (Hi) exchange [mûr]

(I) מְחִיר equivalent value, market price [məḥîr]

מִלֻּאִים consecration, ordina-tion [mil/lu!/ʼîm]

מִקְנָה acquisition [miq/nấ]

נֹגֵן (Qal part) musician, string-player; (Pi) play a stringed instrument [nō/g̠án]

סַל basket [sal]

(II) עָצַב find fault with, hurt [ʽā/ṣáb̠]

עֵקֶב (to the) end; reward; (conj) because (of) [ʽé/qeb̠]

עֲרָפֶל darkness, gloom [ʽărā/p̄él]

עָרַץ be afraid, alarmed [ʽā/ráṣ]

עָשׂוֹר (group of) ten [ʽā/śôr]

עֹשֶׁק oppression [ʽṓ/šeq]

פּוּחַ (v) blow, blast [pûªḥ]

פָּצָה open up [pā/ṣấ]

צִיץ ; צִיצָה (s m; f) blossom (I); (artificial) flower (II) [ṣîṣ; ṣî/ṣấ]

(I) צֶלֶם image [ṣé/lem]

צֶמֶד yoke, team; (ext) acre [ṣé/med̠]

צָמַת (v) silence; (Ni) be silenced [ṣā/mat]

קָדַד bow down, kneel down [qā/d̠ád]

(II) קָצַר be (too) short [qā/ṣár]

רָוָה drink one's fill [rā/wấ]

רֹמַח (pl) lances [rṓ/maḥ]

רְמִיָּה slackness (I?); deceit (II?) [rəmiy/yấ]

(I) שִׁבֹּלֶת ear (of grain), bunch of twigs [šib/bṓ/let]

(I) *שׁוּר gaze on, regard [šûr*]

שָׁעָה look, gaze [šā/ʿấ]

שֶׁרֶץ (coll) swarming things, swarm [šé/reṣ]

תֹּאַר form, shape [tṓ/ʾar]

תָּם (adj) complete, right, peaceful [tām]

תַּנּוּר oven, furnace [tan/nûr]

תַּנִּין; תַּנִּים sea monster [tan/nîn; tan/nîm]

תְּרָפִים idols, household gods [tərā/p̄ǐm]

X. *Words Occurring 14 Times (68)*

אֵזוֹר waistcloth, loincloth [ʾē/zṓr]

(I) אֵיתָן (adj, n) perennial; (met) constant [ʾê/tān]

אָנַף be angry [ʾā/náp̄]

בּוּז show contempt for, despise [bûz]

(III) בַּר grain [bar]

בָּרִיא fat [bā/rîʾ]

גְּאֻלָּה right (duty) of redemption [gə/ʾul/lấ]

גָּבִיעַ (drinking) bowl, cup [gā/b̄îᵃʿ]

גָּעַר (v) reproach [gā/ʿár]

דֶּגֶל banner [dé/ḡel]

דַּק (adj) scanty, fine [daq]

דֶּשֶׁא grass [dé/šeʾ]

(I) הָמַם confuse, disturb [hā/mám]

זוּ (dem and rel pr; c) this [zû]

(I) חוֹתָם (n) seal [ḥô/tắm]

חָכָה await [ḥā/k̠ấ]

חַלָּה (ring-shaped) bread [ḥal/lấ]

טוּל (Hi) throw [ṭûl]

יַבָּשָׁה dry land [yab/bā/šấ]

יָגוֹן torment, grief [yā/ḡṓn]

יְרֻשָּׁה property [yəruš/šấ]

(II) כָּבֵד liver; (liver-) divination [kā/b̄éd]

כְּהֻנָּה priesthood [kəhun/nấ]

(I) כָּרָה excavate, dig [kā/rấ]

(I) כַּרְמֶל orchard [kar/mél]

(II) לָוָה borrow; (Hi) lend to [lā/wấ]

לַפִּיד torch; (ext) lightning [lap/pǐd]

מָחַץ dash, beat to pieces [mā/ḥáṣ]

מִכְשׁוֹל offense, obstacle [mik̠/šṓl]

(I) מָן manna [mān]

(II) מַעֲרָב sunset, west [ma!/ʿəráb̠]

מְצִלָּה*; מְצִלְתַּיִם (pl) bell; (du) cymbals [məṣil/lấ*; məṣil/tá/yim]

מָרַט pluck (hair) [mā/ráṭ]

מַשְׂכִּיל (type of) psalm [maś/kîl]

נְגִינָה string music [nəḡî/nấ]

נֶתֶק a skin disease [né/teq]

סָתַם plug up, stop up [sā/tám]

(I) עֶגְלָה heifer [ʿeḡ/lấ]

עֲדִי (s and coll) ornament(s) [ʿăḏî]

עָכַר (make) trouble; make (someone) taboo? [ʿā/ḵár]

עָצֵל (adj) slow, sluggish [ʿā/ṣḗl]

עָקֵב heel [ʿā/qḗḇ]

עָרָה (Ni) be poured out; (Pi) empty out [ʿā/râ]

פָּגַשׁ meet [pā/ḡáš]

פִּסֵּחַ (adj) lame [pis/sḗªḥ]

פְּעֻלָּה work, deeds; reward, wages [pəʿul/lấ]

פֶּרֶד mule [pé/reḏ]

פָּרַס break [pā/rás]

פַּת bit, morsel [paṯ]

צָבָא go to war, serve [ṣā/ḇắ]

(II) צְבִי gazelle (species) [ṣəḇî]

(I) צַיִד game; hunting [ṣá/yiḏ]

צַעַד walking; (pl) steps [ṣá/ʿaḏ]

קְבוּרָה burial, grave [qəḇû/râ]

קֶמַח flour [qé/maḥ]

קָצַץ cut off, trim [qā/ṣáṣ]

קֶשֶׁר conspiracy [qé/šer]

רָוַח feel relieved; (Hi) smell, enjoy the smell of [rā/wáḥ]

רִיק, רֵק (adj) empty [rêq, rēq]

רָעֵב (stat) be hungry [rā/ʿḗḇ]

(II) שִׂיחַ (object of) concern, interest [śíªḥ]

שְׁאֵלָה request [šəʾē/lấ]

שָׁאַף gasp, pant (for) [šā/ʾáp̄]

שָׁרַץ swarm, teem [šā/ráṣ]

(II) תּוֹר turtledove [tôr]

תּוֹשָׁב sojourner, alien [tô/šáḇ]

(I) תַּחַשׁ porpoise? dolphin? [tá/ḥaš]

תַּן (pl) jackal [tan]

Y. Words Occurring 13 Times (63)

אָנָּא (imprec) please! I pray! [ʾān/nắ]

אָרַג weave; (Qal part) weaver [ʾā/ráḡ]

בָּחִיר (adj) chosen, elect [bā/ḥîr]

(II) בַּת bath (liquid measure) [baṯ]

גֹּדֶל greatness [gṓ/ḏel]

גָּדֵר (stone) wall [gā/ḏḗr]

גְּוִיָּה body [gəwiy/yấ]

דָּקַק crush [dā/qáq]

(II) הַוָּה (n) ruin [haw/wấ]

הָלְאָה (adv) out there, onward [hā/ləʾâ]

וָו (pl) nail [wāw]

זֵד (adj) arrogant [zēḏ]

זוֹב (mucous or blood) discharge [zôḇ]

זָמַם think, plan [zā/mám]

זְנוּנִים prostitution [zənû/nîm]

חָבַק embrace [ḥā/báq]

חָזֶה chest (of animal) [ḥā/zéh]

חַנּוּן (adj) gracious, friendly [ḥan/nûn]

חָנֵף (adj) godless [ḥā/nép̄]

(I) חֹר* (pl) noble [ḥōr*]

טָהֳרָה (cultic) purity [ṭo!/hŏrấ]

טִיט wet clay, mud [ṭîṭ]

טַֿעַם (n) taste [ṭá/ʿam]

יְבוּל (n) produce [yəḇûl]

יָלִיד son; one born a slave [yā/lîd]

יְשִׁימוֹן desert, wilderness [yəšî/môn]

(IV) כֹּֿפֶר bribe [kṓ/p̄er]

לוּלֵא; לוּלֵי (conj) if not [lû/léʾ; lû/lê]

לֻלָאֹת loops [lu!/lā/ʾṓṭ]

מַבּוּל flood [mab/bûl]

מוֹסָד foundation (-wall), base [mô/sắd]

מַחְמָד (something) desirable [maḥ/mắd]

מַחְסוֹר (n) want, need [maḥ/sôr]

מָנָה portion, part, share [mā/nấ]

(II) מַעְגָּל track, rut [maʿ/gál]

מֵֿצַח forehead [mḗ/ṣaḥ]

מִרְעֶה pasture [mir/ʿéh]

(I) מַרְפֵּא healing [mar/pḗʾ]

נְבָלָה stupidity [nəḇā/lấ]

נָעִים (adj) pleasant, lovely [nā/ʿîm]

(II) עָטַף grow weak, faint [ʿā/ṭáp̄]

(II) פָּאַר* (Pi) glorify [pā/ʾár*]

פֶּֿלֶא (n) marvel [pé/leʾ]

פְּנִֿימָה (adv) into, inside [pənî/mấ]

פָּקִיד officer [pā/qîd]

צָחַק laugh; (Pi) joke, play [ṣā/ḥáq]

צְפַרְדֵּֿעַ (coll) frogs [ṣəp̄ar/dḗaʿa]

קָבַב curse [qā/ḇáḇ]

קָבַל* (Pi) accept, receive [qā/ḇál*]

(I) קָו; קַו (measuring-) cord [qāw; qaw]

קַל (adj) light, quick [qal]

קֵן nest; (pl) compartments [qēn]

רָגַע (intrans) crust over, come to rest [rā/ḡáʿ]

רַחוּם (adj) compassionate [ra!/ḥúm]

שְׂרֵפָה (place of) burning, conflagration [śərē/p̄ấ]

שׁוֹאָה (trad) ruin, storm; (better) pit [šô/ʾấ]

(I) שׁוּט* roam about, rove [šûṭ*]

שְׁחִין boil, ulcer [šəḥîn]

(II) שָׁחַר be intent on; (Pi) seek [šā/ḥár]

שִׁכּוֹר (adj) drunk(en) [šik/kôr]

שָׁלַל (v) plunder, spoil [šā/lál]

תָּא guardroom [tāʾ]

תַּֿעַר razor, knife [tá/ʿar]

Z. *Words Occurring 12 Times (78)*

אַדֶּרֶת splendor; robe [ʾad/dé/reṯ]

(II) אַיִן (interr) (from) where? [ʾá/yin]

אָנַח* (Ni) sigh, groan [ʾā/náḥ*]

אֹפֶה baker [ʾō/p̄éh]

בַּהֶרֶת white patch of skin [ba!/hé/reṯ]

(I) בּוּז contempt [bûz]

בּוּס* trample down [bûs*]

בִּי (formula to open conversation with superiors; lit "on me") [bî]

(I) גַּב something arched; torus, boss [gaḇ]

(?) גְּדוּלָה greatness [gəḏûl/lã̂]

(III) גּוּר* be afraid (of) [gûr*]

(I) גָּזַר cut; decide [gā/zár]

גֻּלְגֹּלֶת skull [gul/gó/leṯ]

דֹּב (n; c) bear [dōḇ]

זָעַם (v) curse, scold [zā/ʿám]

חָבֵר (m) companion [ḥā/ḇér]

(II) חַיָּה life; greed, appetite [ḥay/yã̂]

חֲלִיפָה change, relief [ḥălî/p̄ã̂]

חָלָק (adj) smooth [ḥā/láq]

(III) חֹמֶר *homer* (dry measure) [ḥó/mer]

חָפָה (v) cover, veil [ḥā/p̄ã̂]

חָפֵץ having pleasure in; willing [ḥā/p̄éṣ]

חֵקֶר searching [ḥé/qer]

חֹשֵׁב weaver, technician [ḥō/šéḇ]

(I) טֶבַח slaughtering [ṭé/ḇaḥ]

טוּחַ* (v) plaster, overlay [ṭûᵃḥ*]

יוֹנֵק suckling; infant [yô/néq]

יָחִיד (adj) only [yā/ḥîḏ]

(I) יֶרַח (lunar) month [yé/raḥ]

כַּמָּה, כַּמֶּה (interr pr) how much? how many? [kam/-mã̂, kam/méh]

(I) כַּר ram; battering-ram [kar]

לְבֵנָה brick; paving-stone [ləḇē/nã̂]

לַהַב flame [lá/haḇ]

(I) לָוָה accompany; (Ni) be joined, join [lā/wã̂]

לַחַץ oppression, affliction [lá/ḥaṣ]

(I) מִבְחָר (the) choicest, best [miḇ/ḥár]

מֶגֶד yield of fruit; (f pl) precious gifts [mé/ḡed]

מַד clothing, garment [mad]

מְהוּמָה confusion, panic [məhû/mã̂]

מוֹטָה yoke, collar; carrying poles? [mô/ṭã̂]

מוֹסֵר fetter(s), chain(s) [mô/sér]

מוֹרָא fear, terror [mô/rá̓]

מַסַּע breaking (camp), departure [mas/sáʿ]

מְצוֹלָה deep, depths [məṣô/lã̂]

מִצְנֶפֶת headband, turban [miṣ/né/p̄eṯ]

מִקְצוֹעַ corner [miq/ṣôᵃʿ]

מֹר myrrh [mōr]
מַרְאָה vision [mar/'ā]
מְשׁוּבָה* defection [məšû/bā*]
מָתוֹק sweet [mā/tôq]
נָזַר dedicate oneself (to a deity) [nā/zár]
נָפַח (v) blow [nā/páḥ]
(I) נְצִיב pillar; garrison [nəṣîb]
(I) נָשַׁךְ bite [nā/šák]
נֶשֶׁךְ interest (on debt) [né/šek]
נֶשֶׁף twilight, darkness [né/šep]
נֵתַח piece (of meat) [né/taḥ]
סָעַד support, sustain [sā/'ád]
(?) עָוַת pervert; (Pi) make crooked, falsify (I עוּת?) ['ā/wát]
עָמִית fellow, comrade ['ā/mît]
עָקָר (adj) barren ['ā/qár]
(I) עֹרֵב raven ['ō/réb]
פֶּטֶר; פִּטְרָה firstborn [pé/ṭer; piṭ/rā]

צֶמַח (coll) growth, what sprouts [ṣé/maḥ]
קָדְקֹד crown of head [qod/qód]
קוֹץ thorn bush [qôṣ]
קָצִין leader [qā/ṣîn]
רֹאֶה seer; (seeing) visions [rō/'éh]
(II) רֹאשׁ poisonous plant; (ext) poison [rō'š]
(II) רָבַע (den; Qal part pass) squared [rā/bá']
רַגְלִי foot soldier [rag/lî]
רִיק (n) emptiness; (adj) empty, worthless [rîq]
רִקְמָה fabric (of varied colors) [riq/mā]
שָׁסָה (v) plunder; (Qal part) plunderer [šā/sā]
שָׁרַק (v) whistle [šā/ráq]
תּוּשִׁיָּה success [tû/šiy/yā]
תִּיכוֹן (adj) the middle [tî/kôn]
(I) תָּמָר date palm [tā/már]

AA. Words Occurring 11 Times (64)

אֲבָל (interj) truly; (advs conj) but, however ['ăbāl]
אֲנָחָה (n) sigh, groan ['ănā/ḥā]
אִסָּר vow of abstinence ['is/sár]
אָרַשׂ* (Pi, Pu) become engaged ['ă/ráś*]
אֶתְנַן gift ['et/nán]
בָּדָד solitude; (adv) alone [bā/dád]

(II) גָּאַל* (Ni) become polluted [gā/'ál*]
גָּזִית hewn stone, ashlar [gā/zît]
(I) גֵּרָה cud [gē/rā]
דָּקַר pierce [dā/qár]
דָּשֵׁן (stat) become fat [dā/šén]
הָדַף shove [hā/dáp]
הֲלֹם (adv) (to) here [hălōm]

זָדוֹן arrogance [zā/ḏôn]

זַךְ (adj) pure [zak]

זָנָב tail; (met) end [zā/náḇ]

(I) חֹחַ thorn bush, thorn [ḥôªḥ]

חָמוֹת mother-in-law [ḥā/môṯ]

חָמֵץ something leavened [ḥā/méṣ]

(I) חָנֵף be godless, defiled [ḥā/nāp̄]

חַרְטֹם soothsayer-priest [ḥar/ṭôm]

חָשַׁק (v) love [ḥā/šáq]

טָבַח (v) slaughter [ṭā/ḇáḥ]

טָעַם taste, eat [ṭā/ʿám]

יִדְּעֹנִי spirit of the dead; soothsayer [yid/dəʿō/nî]

יָקַץ (intrans) awake, wake up [yā/qáṣ]

יָקַר be difficult; be valued; be precious, rare [yā/qár]

יֹתֶרֶת (extra) lobes of (animal) liver; (met) what is redundant [yō/ṯé/reṯ]

כָּנַס gather, collect [kā/nás]

לָבִיא (poet) lioness [lā/ḇîʾ]

לָהַט consume, burn (I?); (Pi) devour (II?) [lā/háṭ]

(II) *מָגוּר (pl) sojourning; alien citizenship [mā/ḡôr*]

מְחִתָּה terror [məḥit/tâ]

מְצָד stronghold [məṣáḏ]

(I) נֵבֶל (storage-) jar [né/ḇel]

נָבַע (v) bubble (brook) [nā/ḇáʿ]

(II) נָעַר shake [nā/ʿár]

סֹלְלָה siege mound, rampart [sō/lălâ]

סַפִּיר lapis lazuli [sap/pîr]

עוֹלֵל child [ʿô/lél]

עָזַז be strong, prevail [ʿā/záz]

עָמַל labor, exert oneself [ʿā/mál]

עָנַן (Pi) cause to appear, conjure up [ʿā/nán]

עֲצָרָה; עֲצֶרֶת festive assembly [ʿăṣā/rấ; ʿăṣé/reṯ]

(I) עִקֵּשׁ (adj) perverted [ʿiq/qéš]

עָרוּם (adj) subtle, crafty [ʿā/rûm]

פִּתּוּחַ engraving [pit/tûªḥ]

פָּתִיל thread, cord [pā/ṯîl]

צֶאֱצָא (pl) offspring [ṣeʾ!/ʾĕṣâʾ]

(I) *צוּק (Hi) press hard, oppress [ṣûq*]

(I) קָדֵשׁ (adj) consecrated; (n) cult prostitute [qā/ḏéš]

קֶסֶם divination [qé/sem]

קָרֵב (adj) approaching [qā/réḇ]

קָרְחָה baldness [qor/ḥâ]

רִבּוֹ; רִבּוֹא countless; ten thousand [rib/bô; rib/bôʾ]

(I) רָעַם (v) storm, thunder [rā/ʿám]

רָקַע stamp; (Pi) hammer out [rā/qáʿ]

שַׁאֲנָן (adj) at ease, tranquil [ša!/ʾănán]

שַׁבָּתוֹן sabbath feast [šab/bā/ṯôn]

שֹׁהַם (I) onyx? carnelian? lapis lazuli? [šō/hám]

שׁוּל* (pl) flowing skirt; hem of skirt [šûl*]

שַׁוְעָה cry for help [šaw/'â]

שֶׁקֶץ (cultic) abomination [šé/qeṣ]

שָׁתַל plant, transplant [šā/tál]

BB. *Words Occurring 10 Times (67)*

אִגֶּרֶת (official, commercial) letter ['ig/gé/ret]

אֹדוֹת (prep) on account of; (conj) because ['ō/dôt]

אָדַם be red; (Pu part) dyed red ['ā/dám]

אוּץ* urge, be in a hurry; (Hi) urge ['ûṣ*]

אֵזוֹב hyssop? ['ē/zôb]

אֵל (VI) (dem pr) these ['ēl]

אַלּוֹן (I) terebinth, tall tree ['ē/lôn]

אֲפֵלָה darkness ['ăpē/lâ]

בִּגְלַל on account of, for the sake of [biḡ/lál]

בֶּדֶק chink; leak (in ship) [bé/deq]

בִּזָּה plunder (act and objects of) [biz/zâ]

בְּכֹרָה right of firstborn [bəkō/râ]

בַּלָּהָה sudden terror [bal/lā/hâ]

בְּמוֹ (prep) in, by [bəmô]

בְּתוּלִים virginity; evidence of virginity [bətû/lîm]

גְּבוּלָה boundary, territory [gəbû/lâ]

גָּדַר erect a wall [gā/dár]

גָּלָל (II) Cf בִּגְלָל [gā/lál]

גָּעַל abhor [gā/'ál]

גָּעַשׁ shake [gā/'áš]

הַלָּז; הַלָּזֶה (dem pr, m and f; m) this [hal/láz; hal/lā/zéh]

הֶרֶג; הֲרֵגָה (s m; f) killing, murder; slaughter [hé/reḡ; hărē/ḡâ]

זִיד* treat insolently [zîd*]

זֵר molding [zēr]

חָבַל (II) treat badly [ḥā/bál]

חָדַשׁ* (Pi) make new, restore [ḥā/dáš*]

חֲלָצַיִם (du) loins [ḥălā/ṣá/yim]

חֶמְאָה curdled milk [ḥem/'â]

חָרֵב (adj) dry, waste [ḥā/rḗb]

חָרַץ (I) (idiom) threaten; settle, determine [ḥā/ráṣ]

טָבַע sink in [ṭā/bá']

יִתְרוֹן outcome, profit [yit/rôn]

כַּבִּיר strong, powerful [kab/bîr]

כֶּלֶא confinement; prison [ké/le']

מִלּוֹא terrace? (construction) fill? [mil/lô']

מִמְכָּר selling, sale [mim/kár]

מִסְתָּר hiding place [mis/tár]

מַצָּב post (of duty) [maṣ/ṣáb]

מָקַק* (Ni) rot [mā/qáq*]

מִקְרֶה happening, occurrence [miq/réh]

מְרַאֲשׁוֹת head place [məra!/ʾăšôt]

מַרְעִית pasturage [mar/ʿît]

נָגַח (v) gore [nā/ḡáḥ]

נָגַר* (Ni) flow, gush forth [nā/ḡár*]

נָהַל* (Pi) lead, guide [nā/hál*]

נְחוּשָׁה copper, bronze [nəḥû/šáʾ]

נֶשֶׁק, נֵשֶׁק armor, weaponry [nḗ/šeq, né/šeq]

עֵירֹם (adj) naked; (n) nakedness [ʿê/rṓm]

עָנַג* (Pu part) pampered, spoiled; (Hith) pamper oneself [ʿă/náḡ*]

עַפְעַפִּים (du) eyelids?; rays; flashing glance of the eye [ʿap̄/ʿap/-pá/yim]

עֲרֵמָה heap [ʿărē/máʾ]

עֶרֶשׂ bedstead, couch [ʿé/reś]

פָּזַר (Qal part pass) dispersed; (Pi) disperse, scatter [pā/zár]

פַּחַת pit [pá/ḥat]

(I) פֶּלֶג canal [pé/leḡ]

פֶּרֶא wild ass, onager? zebra? [pé/reʾ]

פָּרַק tear away [pā/ráq]

צָמֵא (stat) be thirsty [ṣā/méʾ]

(I) קַדְמֹנִי (adj) eastern [qad/mō/nî]

קָמָה standing grain [qā/máʾ]

קֶרֶס* (pl) hook [qé/res*]

שָׂבֵעַ (adj) full, satisfied [śā/ḇēaʿ]

שָׁמֵן (adj) fat [šā/mḗn]

(I) שְׁפִי barrenness, baldness [šəp̄î]

שְׁרִרוּת hardness, stubbornness [šəri/rût]

תַּהְפּוּכָה* (pl) perversity [tah/-pû/kâ*]

תְּמוּנָה form, image [təmû/náʾ]

SECTION 6: ARAMAIC VOCABULARY (648)

A. *Words Occurring More Than 50 Times (15)*

אֱדַיִן (adv) then ['ĕdá/yin] 57

אֱלָהּ §god; God ['ĕlāh] 95

אֲמַר ‡say; command ['ămar] 73

בְּ־ †(pref prep) in, through, by (means of), for 50

דִּי ; דְּ־ (rel particle) what, that which [dî] 292

הֲוָה §be, happen, exist [hăwâ] 70

וְ־ †(pref conj) and, also, even 50

כְּ־ †(pref prep) like, as 70

כֹּל †all, whole [kōl] 82

לְ־ †(pref prep) for, to 70

לָא ; לָהּ ‡(adv) not [lā'; lâ] 70

מֶלֶךְ †king [mé/lek̲] 178

מַלְכוּ §kingship; kingdom [mal/k̲û] 57

מִן †(prep) from, out of [min] 100

עַל †(prep) on, upon; against; toward; concerning ['al] 98

B. *Words Occurring 50 through 20 Times (27)*

אֱנָשׁ (sg def coll) mankind ['ĕnāš] 25

אֲרַע (the) earth; (ext) inferior ['ăra'] 21

בַּיִת †house; (ext) temple [bá/yit̲] 44

בְּנָה ‡build [bǝnâ] 22

גְּבַר ‡man [gǝb̲ar] 21

דְּהַב gold [dǝhab̲] 23

דְּנָה (dem pr m; adj) this [dǝnâ] 42

חֲזָה ‡see, perceive [ḥăzâ] 31

חֵיוָה beast, animal [ḥê/wâ] 20

חֵלֶם §dream [ḥé/lem] 22

טְעֵם ‡understanding, good sense; report [ṭǝ'ēm] 30

יְדַע ‡know [yǝda'] 47

יְהַב ‡give [yǝhab̲] 28

מִלָּה †word [mil/lâ] 24

עֲבַד ‡do, make ['ăb̲ad̲] 28

עַד †(prep) up to, until; (conj) until ['ad̲] 34

עִם †(prep) with ['im] 22

עֲנָה ‡answer; (ext) begin to speak ['ănâ] 30

פַּרְזֶל §iron [par/zél] 20

פְּשַׁר ‡interpretation [pǝšar] 31

קֳבֵל (prep) before, in front of [qŏb̲ēl] 29

קֳדָם ‡(prep) before, in front of [qŏd̲ām] 42

קוּם ‡*stand (rise) up [qûm*] 35

†רַב (adj) great; chief [rab] 23

†*שִׂים set, lay, put [śîm*] 26

§שָׁמַיִן heaven, sky [šəmá/yin] 38

‡שְׁנָה be different, diverse [šanâ] 21

C. Words Occurring 19 through 13 Times (34)

אִיתַי existence; there is (are) ['î/tái] 17

אִלֵּךְ (dem pr) these ['il/lḗk] 14

§אֲנָה (pers pr) I ['ănâ] 16

אַנְתָּה (pers pr, m s) you ['an/tấ] 15

‡אֲתָה come ['ătâ] 16

‡גַּו, גּוֹ interior [gaw, gô] 13

דֵּךְ, דָּךְ (dem adj, s m; f) that [dēk, dāk] 13

†דָּת decree; state law, law [dāt] 14

†הוּא (pers pr) he; (dem adj) that [hû'] 14

‡הֵיכַל palace; temple [hê/kál] 13

†הֵן (conj) if; whether [hēn] 15

חַד one [ḥad] 14

‡*חֲוָה (Pa, Ha) make known [ḥăwâ*] 15

§חַכִּים (adj) wise (man) [ḥak/kîm] 14

‡יַד hand; (ext) power [yad] 17

†יוֹם day [yôm] 15

‡כְּסַף silver [kəsap] 13

כְּעַן now [kə'an] 13

מָה; †‡מָא (interr pr) what?; (rel pr) what, that which [mâ; mā'] 14

‡נְהַר stream, river [nəhar] 15

נוּר fire [nûr] 17

‡עֲבַר the opposite bank (i.e., west of the Euphrates) ['ăbar] 14

†עֲלַל go in ['ălal] 14

§עָלַם remote time, eternity ['ă/lám] 19

†עַם (coll) people ['am] 15

‡צְלֵם statue [ṣəlēm] 17

§קַדִּישׁ (adj) holy [qad/dîš] 13

†קֶרֶן horn [qé/ren] 14

‡רֵאשׁ head; beginning [rē'š] 14

†שַׂגִּיא (adj) great; much, many; (adv) very [śag/gî'] 13

‡*שְׁכַח (Ha) find [šəkaḥ*] 18

‡שְׁלַח send [šəlaḥ] 14

שָׁלְטָן lordship, dominion [šol/ṭán] 14

תְּלָת; תְּלָתִין (m) three; (pl) thirty [təlāt; təlā/tîn] 13

D. Words Occurring 12 through 10 Times (29)

אָחֳרָן; אָחֳרִי (s m; f) another ['ā/ḥŏrán; 'ā/ḥŏrî] 11

†אַרְיֵה lion ['ar/yéh] 10

אַתּוּן furnace ['at/tûn] 10

‡*בְּהַל (Pa) frighten; (Hithpe) hurry [bəhal*] 11

†*בֵּן (pl) son (cf II בַּר, 6.E) [bēn*] 11

‡בְעָה seek, request [bə'â] 12

‡גֹּב pit [gōb] 10

דְּקַק ‡ break into pieces [dəqaq] 10

הֵמֹון§ ; הִמֹּו (pers pr m) they, them [him/mô; him/môn] 12

זְמָן† time [zəmān] 11

חֵזוּ vision; appearance [ḥĕzû] 12

יְכֵל ‡ (stat) be able; overpower [yəkil] 12

כְּתָב† writing, inscription; document; rule [kətāb] 12

מְדִינָה province [mədî/nâ] 11

מַן ‡ (interr pr) who? (rel pr) whoever [man] 10

נְפַל ‡ fall (down) [nəpal] 11

נְפַק go out [nəpaq] 11

סְגִד ‡ pay homage (to) [səğid] 12

עִדָּן time ['id/dăn] 12

עֲלָי superior, highest; (ext) most high God ['il/lăi] 10

פֶּחָה† governor [pe!/ḥâ] 10

פְּלַח ‡ serve (God) [pəlaḥ] 10

צְבָה long to, desire to [ṣəbâ] 10

קְרָא ‡ shout; read [qərā'] 11

רוּחַ† wind; spirit [rûᵃḥ] 11

רְמָה ‡ throw; place; impose [rəmâ] 12

שְׁאָר† remainder, rest [šə'ār] 12

שַׁלִּיט† (adj) mighty, powerful [šal/lît] 10

שֻׁם ‡ name [šum] 12

E. *Words Occurring 9 and 8 Times (29)*

אַב ‡ father ['ab] 9

אֶבֶן† stone ['é/ben] 8

אֲחַשְׁדַּרְפַּן* (pl) satrap ['ăḥaš/-dar/pán*] 9

אֻמָּה† nation(s) ['um/mâ] 8

אַרְבַּע*† (f) four ['ar/bá'*] 8

אֲתַר ; בַּ(א)תַר trace, place; (prep) in place (of), after ['ătar; bā( )/tár] 8

(I) בַּר† field [bar] 8

(II) בַּר† son (cf בֶּן, 6.D) [bar] 8

גְּלָה ‡† reveal; (Ha) deport [gəlâ] 9

חָכְמָה† wisdom [ḥok/mâ] 8

חֲסַף (formed) clay [ḥăsap] 9

יְקַד burn [yəqad] 8

יַתִּיר (adj) extraordinary; (adv) extremely [yat/tîr] 8

כָּהֵן ‡ priest [kā/hĕn] 8

כֵּן† (adv) thus, so [kēn] 8

כַּשְׂדָּי Chaldean(s); (ext) astrologers [kaś/dái] 9

כְּתַב ‡ write [kətab] 8

לֵב ; לְבַב ‡ heart [lēb; ləbab] 8

מְטָא extend, reach [məṭā'] 8

נְחָשׁ§ copper, bronze [nəḥāš] 9

סְלִק ‡ go (come) up [səliq] 8

עֲדָה ‡ go (away) ['ădâ] 9

קְרֵב ‡ approach, step up to [qərēb] 9

קִרְיָה†‡ town, city [qir/yâ] 9

רַבְרְבָן* (pl) lord, noble [rab/rəbán*] 8

רָז secret [rāz] 9

שֵׁיזֵב (loanword) rescue, save [šê/zíḇ] 9

‡שְׁמַע hear; (Hithpa) obey [šəmaʿ] 9

תּוּב return [tûḇ] 8

F. Words Occurring 7 Times (27)

‡אֲבַד go to ruin, perish [ʾăḇad]

‡אֲזַל go (away) [ʾăzal]

‡אֲכַל eat [ʾăkal]

אָסְפַּרְנָא (adv) exactly, eagerly [ʾos/pár/nāʾ]

‡אֱסָר interdict [ʾĕsār]

†*דּוּר live, dwell [dûr*]

†הִיא (pers pr) she [hîʾ]

‡הֲלַךְ go [hălak]

†חַי (adj) living, alive; (pl) life [ḥai]

†חַיִל strength; army [ḥá/yil]

יְקָר honor, majesty [yəqār]

‡*כְּלַל (Shaphel) finish [kəlal*]

†*כְּנָת (pl) colleague [kənāṯ*]

(II) לָהֵן (conj) unless, except;

(advs) but, but rather [lā/hḗn]

§לְשָׁן tongue; (ext) language [liš/šán]

‡מְאָה hundred [məʾâ]

מָאן (pl) vessel [māʾn]

‡נְתַן give [nəṯan]

עֲבֵד servant [ʿăḇḗḏ]

‡עֲשַׂר; עֶשְׂרִין (m) ten; (pl) twenty [ʿăśar; ʿeś/rîn]

‡קְטַל kill [qəṭal]

§קָל voice; sound [qāl]

‡*רְגַל (du) foot [rəḡal*]

‡רְשַׁם write [rəšam]

‡שְׁלֵט rule; overpower [šəlēṭ]

(I) ‡שְׁנָה year [šənâ]

תּוֹר (pl) bull, ox, steer [tôr]

G. Words Occurring 6 Times (22)

אִילָן tree [ʾî/lán]

‡אָשַׁף conjurer [ʾā/šáp]

‡בְּטֵל (intrans) stop; be discontinued [bəṭēl]

‡גְּזַר (part pl) astrologers; (Hith) be cut out [gəzar]

דְּחַל (part) fear, frightening [dəḥal]

†הֲ־ (pref interr particle)

זִיו brightness [zîw]

‡*חֲבַל (Pa) hurt, injure [ḥăḇal*]

‡חֲיָה (v) live [ḥăyâ]

‡חֲמַר wine [ḥămar]

‡מִשְׁכַּב bed, couch [miš/káḇ]

‡נְחַת come down [nəḥat]

§סָפַר clerk, secretary [sā/pár]

עֲבִידָה work; administration [ʿăḇî/dấ]

פֻּם mouth; (ext) entrance [pum]

†פִּתְגָם word; decree [piṯ/ḡám]

‡רְבָה become great, grow up [rəḇâ]	‡שְׁאֵל ask, desire, require [šəˀēl]
‡רְבִיעָי fourth [rəḇî/ˁái]	‡שְׁבַע seven [šəḇaˁ]
רַעְיוֹן* (pl) thought [raˁ/yôn*]	‡שְׁרָה loosen [šərâ]

H. Words Occurring 5 Times (35)

אֲלוּ (interj) behold! [ˀălû]	‡סְגַן* (pl) prefect, governor [səḡan*]
אִלֵּין (dem pr) these [ˀil/lên]	סוֹף end [sôp̄]
אָע wood [ˀāˁ]	‡סְפַר book [səp̄ar]
אֲרוּ (interj) behold! [ˀărû]	סָרַךְ* (pl) official [sā/rák*]
‡בְּקַר* (Pa) search [bəqar*]	†עַיִן eye [ˁá/yin]
בְּרַם (advs adv) but, yet, only [bəram]	‡עֲשַׂב grass; (coll) greens [ˁăśaḇ]
גְּשֵׁם body [gəšēm]	צְבָע* (Pa) wet, moisten [ṣəḇāˁ*]
דָּא (dem pr f) this [dāˀ]	†רְבוּ greatness [rəḇû]
†דִּין (n) right, judgment; council of judges [dîn]	†רוּם height [rûm]
†חַרְטֹם magician [ḥar/ṭóm]	שָׂב* (pl) elders [śāḇ*]
†טַל dew [ṭal]	‡שְׁבַח* (Pa) praise [šəḇaḥ*]
יַצִּיב (adj) reliable [yaṣ/ṣîḇ]	שְׁבַק leave [šəḇaq]
יְתִב sit down; dwell [yəṯiḇ]	שָׁעָה moment [šā/ˁâ]
כְּנֵמָא (adv) thus, so [kənế/māˀ]	שֵׁת; שִׁתִּין (m) six; (pl) sixty [šēṯ; šit/tîn]
§לֵילִי night [lê/lê]	‡שְׁתָה drink [šəṯâ]
‡מְלַל* (Pa) speak [məlal*]	§תְּחוֹת (prep) under [təḥôṯ]
‡מְנָה count, number [mənâ]	†תַּקִּיף (adj) strong, mighty [taq/qîp̄*]
	†תְּקֵף (stat) be(come) strong [təqip̄]

I. Words Occurring 4 Times (40)

†אַל (neg) not [ˀal]	(II) ‡בְּרַךְ bless [bərak]
†אַמָּה* (pl) cubit [ˀam/mấ*]	גָּלוּ exile [gā/lûˁ]
אִנּוּן (pers pr) they [ˀin/nûn]	הַדָּבַר* (pl) royal official [had/dā/ḇár*]
§אֲנַחְנָא (pers pr) we [ˀáná/ḥanāˀ]	זְמָר (string-) music [zəmār]

†*זַן (pl) kind, sort [zan*]

חֲבֵר*‡; חַבְרָה* (pl m; f) companion [ḥăbar*; ḥab/râ*]

‡חֲלַף pass by (over) [ḥălap̄]

חֲנֻכָּה dedication [ḥănuk/kâ]

טְרַד drive away [ṭərad]

כְּהֵל (stat) be able [kəhēl]

כְּעֶנֶת (adv) and now [kə'é/net]

כְּפַת be bound, tied up [kəp̄at]

מִדָּה tax, tribute [mid/dâ]

מְדוֹר dwelling [mədôr]

מְחָא strike [məḥā']

מַנְדַּע understanding [man/dá']

מָרֵא lord [mã/rḗ']

מַשְׁרוֹקִי pipe (musical instrument) [maš/rô/qî]

‡נְבִיא prophet [nəbî']

‡*נְדַב (Hithpa) bestow; be willing; (part) disposed, willing [nədab*]

§נְזַק (part) suffer loss; (Ha part, inf) wrong, injure [nəzaq]

†*עֶלְיוֹן (pl) the Most High ['el/yṓn*]

עֲנַף (pl) branch, bough ['ănap̄]

‡עֲרַב (Pa) mix ['ărab*]

פְּסַנְתֵּרִין harp [pəsan/tē/rín]

פַּרְשֶׁגֶן copy [par/šé/ḡen]

‡*צְלַח (Ha) cause to prosper; make progress [ṣəlaḥ*]

§צְפַר (pl) bird [ṣip/pár*]

קִיתָרֹס (?) kithara (kind of lyre or lute) [qai/tərós]

†*רוּם raise oneself; (Pol) praise [rûm*]

שַׂבְּכָא lyre? [śab/kắ']

†שָׁלֵה; שָׁלוּ negligence [(Q) šā/lû; šā/lû]

§שְׁלָם well-being, good health, welfare [šəlām]

‡*שְׁפֵל (Ha) bring low, humble [šəp̄ēl*]

תַּמָּה (adv) there [tam/mâ]

תְּרֵין; תַּרְתֵּין (s m; f) two [tərên; tar/tḗn]

J. *Words Occurring 3 Times (66)*

אֵב†; אִנְבָּא (abs; emph) fruit ['ēb; 'in/bắ']

אִגְּרָה§; אִגְּרָא letter (correspondence) ['ig/gərã; 'ig/gərắ]

אֲזָה light a fire, heat ['ăzâ]

†*אַחַר (adv pl) after ['a!/ḥár*]

אֵלֶּה; אֵל†* (dem pl) these ['ēl*; 'ēl/leh]

‡*אֲמַן (Ha) trust in ['ămán*]

אִמַּר (pl) (sacrificial) lamb ['im/már]

‡אֱסוּר bond(s), fetter(s); (pl, ext) imprisonment ['ĕsûr]

†אַף (conj) also ['ap̄]

†*אֶצְבַּע finger; toe ['eṣ/bá'*]

אַרְגְּוָן purple (garment) ['ar/gəwắn]

אֹשׁ (pl def) foundation ['ōš]

§*אָת (pl) sign ['āt*]

בָּאתַר after [bā'/tár]

בְּלוֹ tribute [bəlô]

‡בְּעֵל owner, master, lord [bəˈēl]

‡בְּשַׂר flesh [bəśar]

‡*גְּנַז (pl) treasure [gənaz*]

גַּף (pl) wing [gap̄]

דִּכֵּן (dem pr c) that [dik/kḗn]

דְּכַר (pl) ram [dəkar]

‡*הַדַּר (Pa) glorify [hăḏar*]

‡הֲדַר (n) splendor, majesty [hăḏar]

הֲלָךְ toll duty [hălāḵ]

הַמּוּנָךְ (?) necklace [ham/mû/nák]

חֲבָל hurt, injury [ḥăḇāl]

חֲלָק portion, lot [ḥălāq]

‡*טְעַם (Pa) feed [təˈam*]

‡*יְבַל (Ha) bring [yəḇal*]

יְעַט advise; (part) counselor; (Ithpaal) deliberate [yəˈaṭ]

כְּנַשׁ assemble [kənaš]

כָּרְסֵא seat, throne [kor/sḗ']

‡לְבַשׁ be clothed with [ləḇaš]

(I) †לָהֵן (adv) therefore [lā/hḗn]

לְחֵנָה (pl) concubine [ləḥē/nấ]

‡מְלַח salt [məlaḥ]

מְנֵא mina (unit of weight) [mənē']

‡*מַתְּנָה (pl) gift [mat/tənấ*]

נְוָלוּ garbage heap; dunghill [nəwā/lû']

נְצַל (Ha) deliver, rescue [nəṣal]

‡נְשָׂא take, carry away [nəśā']

†נִשְׁתְּוָן decree [niš/təwán]

סוּמְפֹּנְיָה bagpipe? (musical instrument) [sûm/pō/-nəyấ]

§עִיר watcher; (ext) angel [ˈîr]

עִלָּה pretext [ˈil/lấ]

עֳפִי foliage, leaves [ˈŏp̄î]

‡עִקַּר root(stock) [ˈiq/qár]

עַתִּיק (adj) old, aged [ˈat/tîq]

‡צַוַּאר neck [ṣaw/wáʾr]

‡*קְבַל (Pa) receive [qəḇal*]

קַדְמָי first [qaḏ/mấi]

קְטַר (pl) knot, joint [qəṭar]

‡קְצָת end; part [qəṣāṯ]

‡*רְגַשׁ (Ha) storm in? [rəḡaš*]

§שְׂגָא grow, become great [śəḡấ]

שָׂכְלְתָנוּ insight [śoḵ/ləṯā/nû']

שְׂעַר hair [śəˈar]

שֵׂגַל (pl) concubine [śē/ḡál]

†*שׁוּר (pl) wall [šûr*]

שְׁחַת (part pass) corrupt; (n) mischief [šəḥaṯ]

‡שְׁלִם (stat) be finished [šəlim]

†*שֵׁן (du) tooth [šēn*]

‡שְׁפַר please, seem good [šəp̄ar]

‡*שְׁרֹשׁ (pl) root [šərōš*]

תַּלְתָּא triumvir? third part? [tal/táʾ]

תְּמַהּ (pl) wonder, miracle [təmah]

K. Words Occurring 2 Times (88)

אֲדַרְגָּזַר* (pl only) counselor [ʾăḏar/gā/zár*]

(?) אֲזְדָא (adj f?) promulgated [ʾaz/dáʾ]

‡אֶלַף thousand [ʾăláp̄]

‡*אֲנַף (du) face [ʾănap̄*]

אֲפַרְסְכָי (pl; unc) title of official? [ʾăp̄ar/səḵái]

‡*אֹרַח (pl) way [ʾăraḥ*]

§אַרְכָה length(ening), prolongation [ʾar/ḵáʾ]

(?) אֻשַּׁרְן timber? panelling? roof scaffolding? [ʾiš/rán]

אֶשְׁתַּדּוּר revolt [ʾeš/taḏ/dúr]

†בֵּין (prep) between [bên]

בָּעוּ petition, prayer [bā/ʾû]

†*בַּת (pl) bath (liquid measure) [bat*]

†גְּבוּרָה† strength [gəḇû/ráʾ]

גְּדָבַר (pl) treasurer [gəḏā/ḇár]

‡גְּדַד cut down [gəḏaḏ]

†גְּזֵרָה decree [gəzē/ráʾ]

גְּלָל (coll) blocks of stone [gəlāl]

†דִּבְרָה affair, matter [diḇ/ráʾ]

דָּכְרָן (pl) minutes, memorandum [doḵ/rán]

‡דְּמָה resemble [dəmáʾ]

§דָּר generation [dār]

דֶּתֶא grass [dé/teʾ]

דְּתָבַר (pl n) judge [dəṯā/ḇár]

הַדָּם (pl) member, limb [had/dám]

‡*זוּעַ tremble [zûᵃʿ*]

חֲזוֹת sight [ḥăzôṯ]

חֵמָה rage, fury [ḥămâ]

חִנְטָה (pl) (grains of) wheat [ḥin/ṭâ]

‡חֲנַן show mercy [ḥănan]

‡*חֲסַן (Ha) take possession of, possess [ḥăsan*]

‡חֱסֵן might, wealth? [ḥĕsēn]

חֲצַף (Ha part f) harsh, severe [ḥăṣap̄]

§טָב (adj) good [ṭāḇ]

טוּר mountain [ṭûr]

טִין (wet) clay [ṭîn]

טְפַר (pl) (finger-) nail, claw [ṭəp̄ar]

‡*יְדָה (Ha) praise [yəḏâ*]

‡יַם sea [yam]

יַקִּיר (adj) difficult; noble [yaq/qîr]

‡יְרַח month [yəraḥ]

§כְּתַל wall [kəṯal]

†לְבוּשׁ garment [ləḇûš]

‡מֵאמַר word, order [mē/már]

מָזוֹן food [mā/zôn]

‡מְלָא fill [məláʾ]

‡מַלְאַךְ† angel [mal/ʾáḵ]

†מַלְכָּה queen (-mother) [mal/káʾ]

†מִנְחָה offering [min/ḥáʾ]

מָרָד (adj) rebellious [mā/ráḏ]

מְשַׁח (anointing-) oil [məšaḥ]

נְבִזְבָּה present, gift [nəḇiz/báʾ]

נִדְבָּךְ course (of stones, timber) [niḏ/báḵ]

נַהִירוּ illumination, insight [na!/hî/rû]

‡נְטַל lift up [nəṭal]

נִיחֹוחַ (pl) incense [nî/ḥô°ḥ]

§*נְכַס (pl) treasure, treasury; fine [nəkas*]

נִפְקָה cost [nip̄/qâ]

‡נְשַׁר eagle [nəšar]

‡*סוּף be fulfilled; (Ha) annihilate [sûp̄*]

סַרְבָּל (pl) trousers? tunic? cloak? [sar/bål]

†עֹוף bird; (coll) birds [ʿôp̄]

עִזְקָה signet-ring [ʿiz/qâ]

פַּס hand [pas]

פְּרֵס half(-*shekel*); half (-*mina*)? [pərēs]

§פְּשַׁר interpret [pəšar]

פְּתַח (Pe pass) open(ed) [pətaḥ]

פְּתָי width [pətāi]

†צַד side [ṣad]

צְלָה (Pa) pray [ṣəlâ]

‡קַדְמָה former times [qad/mâ]

קְיָם statute, decree [qəyām]

קַיָּם (adj) enduring [qay/yåm]

קְרַץ (pl) piece; (in idiom) slander [qəraṣ]

‡קְשֹׁט truth [qəšōṭ]

רִבֹּו great number, ten thousand [rib/bô]

רֵו appearance [rēw]

§רְעוּ will, decision [rəʿû]

‡רְעַע shatter [rəʿaʿ]

‡רְפַס trample down [rəpas]

‡שְׁבִיב flame [šəḇîḇ]

‡שְׁוָה be like [šəwâ]

‡שְׁכַן live, dwell [šəkan]

‡*שִׁלְטֹון (pl) high official [šil/ṭôn*]

שַׁפִּיר fair, lovely [šap/pîr]

תְּדִיר duration [tədîr]

תִּפְתָּי (pl) police officer? magistrate? [tip̄/tåi]

תְּקֵל *shekel* (unit of measure and weight) [təqēl]

תְּרַע door, opening; court [təraʿ]

L. *Words Occurring 1 Time (236)*

אִדַּר (pl) threshing-floor [ʾid/dár]

אַדְרַזְדָּא (adv) diligently, zealously [ʾad/raz/då]

אֶדְרָע arm; (met) force [ʾed/rå]

‡*אַח (pl) brother [ʾaḥ*]

אֲחִידָה (pl) riddle [ʾăḥî/dâ]

§אַחֲרִי end [ʾaḥărî]

(?) אַחֲרִין (adv) at last [ʾa!/ḥărîn]

אֵימְתָן (adj) frightful [ʾê/mətån]

‡אֲנַס (part) distress [ʾănas]

אַנְתּוּן (pers pr, m pl) you [ʾan/tûn]

אֲפַרְסִי (pl; unc) gent? title of official? [ʾăp̄ā/rəsái]

אֲפַרְסַתְכָי (pl) title of officials [ʾăp̄ar/sat/kái]

אַפְּתֹם treasury? [ʾap/pətŏm]

אֲרִיךְ fitting [ʾărîk]

אַרְכֻּבָּה (pl) knee [ʾar/kub/-bâ]

אַרְעִי bottom [ʾar/ʿî]

אֲרַק (the) earth [ʾăraq]

אֶשָׁא fire ['eš/šấ']

בְּאִישׁ (f def) evil, bad [bə'îš]

‡בְּאֵשׁ (stat) be bad [bə'ēš]

בְּדַר (Pa) scatter [bədar]

בְּהִילוּ hurry, haste [bəhî/lû']

†בִּינָה insight, discernment [bî/nấ]

בִּירָה citadel, fortress [bî/rấ]

בִּית pass the night [bît]

בָּל heart; (ext) mind [bāl]

‡*בְּלָה (Pa) wear (someone) down [bəlâ*]

†בִּנְיָן building [bin/yán]

בְּנַס become angry [bənas]

†בִּקְעָה plain [biq/'ấ]

(I) ‡בְּרַךְ kneel down [bərak]

‡*בְּרַךְ (pl) knee [bərak*]

גַּב (pl) back? side? [gab]

§*גְּבַר (pl) strong man [gib/bár*]

†גֵּוָה pride [gē/wấ]

§*גּוּחַ (Ha) stir up [gûᵃḥ*]

גִּזְבַּר (pl) treasurer [giz/bár]

§גִּיר (n) plaster [gîr]

†*גַּלְגַּל (pl) wheel [gal/gál*]

‡גְּמַר (part pass) finished [gəmar]

‡*גְּרַם (pl) bone [gəram*]

†דֹּב bear [dób]

דְּבַח (v) sacrifice [dəbaḥ]

דְּבַח (pl n) sacrifice [dəbaḥ]

‡דְּבַק stick (hold) together [dəbaq]

(?) דְּהוּא (text corr?) that is [dəhû']

‡*דּוּשׁ trample down [dûš*]

דַּחֲוָה (pl) food? diversion? [da!/ḥăwâ]

†*דִּין (v) judge [dîn*]

†*דַּיָּן (pl n) judge [day/yán*]

דִּינָיֵא judges [dî/nā/yế']

דִּכְרוֹן minutes, memorandum [dik/rṓn]

‡דְּלַק burn [dəlaq]

דְּרָע (pl) arm [dərāʿ]

‡הָא (interj) behold! [hāʾ]

†הָא(־כְדִי) just as [hēʾ(-kədî)]

הַרְהֹר (pl) dream-fantasies [har/hṓr]

זְבַן buy [zəban]

זְהִיר (pl adj) cautious, careful [zəhîr]

‡*זוּד (Ha) act insolently [zûd*]

זוּן (Hith) feed on, live on [zûn]

§זָכוּ innocence [zā/kû']

‡*זְמַן (Hith) agree [zəman*]

זַמָּר (pl) singer [zam/már]

זְעֵיר (adj) small [zə'êr]

‡זְעִק cry out, shout [zə'iq]

‡זְקַף (part pass) impaled [zəqap]

‡זְרַע (coll) seed; (ext) descendants [zəraʿ]

חֲבוּלָה crime [ḥăbû/lấ]

חֲדֵה (pl) breast [ḥădēh]

†חֶדְוָה joy [ḥed/wấ]

חֲדַת new [ḥădat]

(?) *חוּט repair? inspect? [ḥûṭ*]

חִוָּר white [ḥiw/wár]

§חֲטָי sin [ḥăṭāi]

§חַטָּיָה (K) sin-offering [ḥaṭ/ṭā/yấ]

§ חֲסִיר (adj) defective, of poor quality [ḥas/sîr]

חֲרַב (Ho) be devastated, destroyed [ḥărab]

חֲרַךְ (Hithpa) be singed (by fire) [ḥărak]

§ חֲרַץ hip [ḥăraṣ]

‡ חֲשַׁב reckon, regard [ḥăšab]

§ חֲשׁוֹךְ darkness [ḥăšôk]

חֲשַׁח (v) need [ḥăšaḥ]

חַשְׁחָה (pl n) need [ḥaš/ḥâ]

חַשְׁחוּ (n) need [ḥaš/ḥû]

חֲשַׁל crush, pulverize [ḥăšal]

‡ חֲתַם (v) seal [ḥătam]

טָאֵב (stat) be good [ṭəʼêb]

†*טַבָּח (pl) executioner, bodyguard [ṭab/báḥ*]

טְוָת (n) fasting; (adv) in fasting [ṭəwāt]

§*טְלַל (Ha) make a nest [ṭəlal*]

טַרְפְּלָיֵ (pl) class of officials? [ṭar/pəlăi]

‡ יַבֶּשֶׁה dry land; (def) the earth [yab/bəšâ]

יְגַר heap of stones [yəgar]

‡ יְטַב it suits, pleases [yəṭab]

‡*יְסַף (Ho) be added [yəsap̄*]

יְצָא (Shaphel) finish [yəṣāʼ]

‡*יְצַב (Pa) make certain (of) [yəṣab*]

יְקֵדָה burning [yəqē/dâ]

יַרְכָה (pl) upper thigh [yar/kâ]

יָת (accusative particle; object marker; not translated) [yāt]

כִּדְבָה a lie (falsehood) [kid/bâ]

‡ כָּה (adv) here, hitherto [kâ]

כַּוָּה (pl) window [kaw/wâ]

‡*כַּכַּר (pl) talent (weight) [kak/kár*]

כֹּר, כּוֹר (pl) kor (dry measure) [kōr, kôr*]

כַּרְבְּלָה (pl) cap [kar/bəlâ]

כְּרָה (Ithpeel) be anxious [kərâ]

כָּרוֹז herald [kā/rôz]

כְּרַז (Ha) proclaim [kəraz]

לְוָת (prep) near, beside [ləwāt]

‡ לְחֶם bread; (ext) meal, feast [ləhem]

§ מֹאזְנֵא balance (scales) [mōʼ/zənêʼ]

†מְגִלָּה scroll [məgil/lâ]

‡*מְגַר (Pa) overthrow [məgar*]

מַדְבַּח altar [mad/báḥ]

‡ מוֹת death [môt]

§*מַחְלְקָה (pl) division (of Levites) [maḥ/ləqâ*]

מְלַח eat (the) salt; (idiom) be under obligation of loyalty [məlaḥ]

מְלַךְ (n) counsel [məlak]

מִנְיָן (n) number [min/yán]

†*מַעֲבָד (pl) work [ma!/ʼābād*]

§*מְעֵה (pl) belly [məʻēh*]

מֶעָל (pl) sunset [me!/ʼál]

‡ מְרַד rebellion [mərad]

מְרַט ‡ (?) (stat) be plucked out [mərit]

מִשְׁכַּן ‡ dwelling, abode [miš/kán]

מִשְׁתְּא‡* (drinking-) feast [miš/té']

נְבָא‡* (Hithpa) prophesy [nəbā'*]

נְבוּאָה† prophecy, prophesying [nəbû/'â]

נֶבְרְשָׁה lampstand [neb/rəšâ]

נְגַד ‡ (v) flow [nəḡaḏ]

נֶגֶד† (prep) toward [né/ḡed]

נְגַהּ brightness [nəḡah]

נְדַד ‡ flee [nədaḏ]

נִדְנֶה (n) sheath? body?; (ext) on account of this [nid/néh]

נְהוֹר; נְהִיר (Q; K) light [nəhôr; nəhîr]

נוּד* flee [nûḏ*]

נְטַר keep (in one's heart) [nəṭar]

נְמַר ‡ panther [nəmar]

נְסַח‡* (Hith) be pulled out [nəsaḥ*]

נְסַךְ‡* (Pa) offer [nəsak*]

נְסַךְ* (pl) drink-offering, libation [nəsak*]

נִצְבָּה firmness, hardness [niṣ/bâ]

נְצַח‡* (Hithpa) distinguish oneself [nəṣaḥ*]

נְקֵא§ (adj) pure [nəqē']

נְקַשׁ‡ knock together [nəqaš]

נְשִׁין* (pl) wife [nəšîn*]

נִשְׁמָה‡ breath [niš/mâ]

נְתִין*† (pl) (temple-) slave [nəṯîn*]

נְתַר* (Aphel) shake off

[nəṯar*]

סְבַל‡* (Poel part) be preserved? erect? [səḇal*]

סְבַר§ seek, strive [səḇar]

סְגַר shut [səḡar]

סְעַד‡* (Pa) support [sə'aḏ*]

סְתַר‡* (I) (Pa part pass) hidden things [səṯar*]

סְתַר§ (II) destroy, demolish [səṯar]

עוֹד† (adv) still, yet ['ôḏ]

עֲוָיָה* (pl) offense ['ăwā/yâ*]

עוּר chaff ['ûr]

עֵז* (pl) goat ['ēz*]

עֵטָה counsel ['ē/ṭâ]

עֵלָּה above ['él/lâ]

עֲלָוָה* (?) (pl) burnt offering ['al/wâ*]

עִלִּי† roof chamber ['il/lî]

עֲלַע* (pl) rib ['ăla'*]

עַמִּיק* (pl adj) deep, impenetrable (things) ['am/mîq*]

עֲמַר wool ['ămar]

עֲנֵה* (pl adj) miserable ['ănēh*]

עֲנָן‡* (pl) clouds ['ănān*]

עֲנָשׁ fine (imposed) ['ănāš]

עֲצִיב (adj) sorrowful, afflicted ['ăṣîḇ]

עֲקַר‡* (Ithpeel) be plucked out ['ăqar*]

עָר‡ adversary ['ār]

עֲרָד§* (pl) wild ass, onager? ['ărāḏ*]

עַרְוָה‡ dishonor ['ar/wâ]

עֲשַׁת‡ think, plan ['ăšat]

‡*עָתִיד (pl adj) ready to [ʿātîd*]

פֶּחָר potter [pe!/ḥár]

פַּטִישׁ (pl) garment (coat? trousers?)) [paṭ/ṭîš]

‡פְּלַג (v) divide [pəlaḡ]

‡פְּלַג (n) half [pəlaḡ]

פְּלֻגָּה (pl) division (of priests) [pəlug/gâ]

פָּלְחָן (cultic) service [pol/ḥán]

‡פְּרַס divide [pəras]

‡פְּרַק unloose, abolish [pəraq]

‡*פְּרַשׁ (Pa part pass) separate(ly)? [pəraš*]

צְבוּ thing, matter [ṣəḇû]

צְדָא (interr) is it true? [ṣəḏāʾ]

‡צִדְקָה beneficence, justice [ṣid/qâ]

‡*צְפִיר (pl) he-goat [ṣəpîr*]

קַיְט summer [qá/yiṭ]

‡קְנָה buy [qənâ]

‡קְצַף become furious [qəṣap]

‡קְצַף (n) wrath [qəṣap]

‡*קְצַץ (Pa) cut off [qəṣaṣ*]

†קְרָב war [qərāḇ]

רְגַז (Ha) anger, enrage [rəḡaz]

‡רְגַז (n) rage [rəḡaz]

רַחִיק (pl adj) far [ra!/ḥîq]

§רַחֲמִין compassion [ra!/ḥămîn]

רְחַץ (Hith) rely (on) [rəḥaṣ]

רֵיחַ (n) smell [rêaḥ]

‡רַעֲנַן (adj) prosperous, flourishing [ra!/ʿănan]

שָׂחֲדוּ testimony [śā/ḥăḏû]

שְׂטַר side [śəṭar]

‡*שְׂכַל (Hith) consider [śəkal*]

שָׂנֵא (part) adversary [śənēʾ]

†שְׁאֵלָה question [šəʾē/lâ]

‡*שְׁבַט (pl) tribe [šəḇaṭ*]

שְׁבַשׁ (Hithpa) be perplexed [šəḇaš]

שְׁדַר (Hithpa) be like [šəḏar]

שֵׁיצִיא (loanword; v) finish [šê/ṣîʾ]

§שְׁלֵה (adj) at ease [šəlēh]

‡שְׁלֵוָה prosperity, fortune [šəlē/wâ]

‡*שְׁמַד (Ha) destroy, exterminate [šəmaḏ*]

‡*שְׁמַם (Ithpoel) stiffen with fright [šəmam*]

שְׁמַשׁ (Pa) serve [šəmaš]

‡שְׁמַשׁ sun [šəmaš]

(II) ‡שְׁנָה (n) sleep [šənâ]

‡שְׁפַט (part) judge [šəpaṭ]

‡שְׁפַל low(ly) [šəpal]

שְׁפַרְפָּר dawn [šəpar/pár]

§שָׁק (du) (lower) leg [šāq*]

(?) שֵׁרְשׁוּ banishment, exclusion [šərō/šû]

תְּבַר break [təḇar]

תְּוַה be alarmed [təwah]

תְּלַג snow [təlaḡ]

תְּלִיתָי third [təlî/ṭái]

תִּנְיָן second [tin/yán]

תְּנִינוּת (adv) a second time
[tin/yā/nûṯ]

תָּקַל weigh [təqal]

‡*תְּקַן (Ho) be reestablished
[təqan*]

תְּקָף strength [təqāp̄]

תְּקֹף strength [təqōp̄]

*תָּרָע (pl) doorkeeper
[tā/rā῾*]

INDEX

Hebrew and Aramaic words are indexed separately. Verbs are given no vowel points. Other words are also unpointed, except for forms with identical consonantal spelling. Root numbers in parentheses differentiate between identical spellings with different meanings. References are to Section number (1-6), and Subsection letter (A-Z, AA, BB). For convenience the number of occurences is also given for Hebrew and Aramaic words.

Index to Hebrew Vocabulary

א

אב 1.B 1568	אוי 5.N 24	אִי (I) 5.G 36
אבד 3.A 183	אויל (I) 5.L 27	איב, אויב 2.C 281
אבה 4.J 54	אולי (II) 5.C 45	איד 5.N 24
אביון 4.H 61	אולם (I) 5.S 19	איה 4.K 52
אבימלך 4.F 67	אולת 5.M 25	איוב 4.H 58
אביר 5.O 23	אָוֶן 4.C 80	אֵיךְ 4.H 60
אבל 5.F 39	און (I) 5.T 18	איכה 5.V 16
אֵבֶל 5.N 24	אופן 5.H 35	איל (I) 3.B 161
אֱבָל 5.AA 11	אוץ 5.BB 10	איל (III) 5.P 22
אבן 2.D 268	אוצר 4.C 79	אַיל 5.P 22
אבנר 4.G 63	אור 5.D 43	אילם; אולם 4.K 50
אברהם; אברם 2.D 235	אוֹר 3.E 125	אימה 5.U 17
אבשלום 3.G 107	אות (I) 4.C 79	אין (I) 1.C 773
אגרת 5.BB 10	אז; מאז 3.D 141	אין (II) 5.Z 12
אדום; אדמי 3.F 112	אזוב 5.BB 10	אֵיפָה 5.F 38
אדון; אדני 1.C 770	אזור 5.X 14	אֵיפֹה 5.M 25
אדות 5.BB 10	אֹזֶן (I) 5.E 41	אִישׁ (I) 1.B 2149
אדיר 5.L 27	אֹזֶן 3.A 187	אֵיתָן (I) 5.X 14
אדם 5.BB 10	אזר 5.V 16	אַךְ 3.B 160
אָדָם (I) 1.D 553	אזרח 5.U 17	אכל 1.C 795
אדמה (I) 2.D 225	אח (II) 1.D 626	אֹכֶל 5.C 45
אדן 4.I 55	אחאב 4.A 93	אכלה 5.T 18
אדרת 5.Z 12	אחד; אחת 1.C 959	אכן 5.T 18
אהב 2.E 205	אחור 5.E 41	אל (I) 1.C 738
אהבה (I) 5.E 40	אחות 3.F 114	אֶל (V) 2.D 236
אהל (I) 2.B 342	אחז (I) 4.G 63	אֶל (VI) 5.BB 10
אהרון 2.B 347	אחזה 4.F 66	אֵל 1.A 5000
או 2.B 311	אחר 5.T 18	אָלָה 5.G 37
אוב (II) 5.V 16	אַחַר (I) 3.B 166	אָלָה (I) 5.V 16
אוה 5.L 27	אַחַר 1.D 713	אֵלֶּה 1.C 738
	אחרון 4.K 50	אלהים (II) 1.A 2706
	אחרית 4.H 61	אלון (I) 5.BB 10
	אי 5.J 31	אלוף 4.F 69

Index to Aramaic Vocabulary